The Ultimate English Literature Admissions Test Guide

UniAdmissions

Published by *RAR Medical Services Limited, trading as* **Infinity Books**
www.uniadmissions.co.uk
info@uniadmissions.co.uk
Tel: +44 (0) 208 068 0438

This book is neither created nor endorsed by Cambridge Assessment. The authors and publisher are not affiliated with Cambridge Assessment, or with the Universities of Oxford or Cambridge. The information offered in this book is purely advisory and any advice given should be taken within this context. As such, the publishers and authors accept no liability whatsoever for the outcome of any applicant's English Literature Admissions Test (ELAT) performance, the outcome of any university applications or for any other loss. Although every precaution has been taken in the preparation of this book, the publisher and author assume no responsibility for errors or omissions of any kind. Neither is any liability assumed for damages resulting from the use of information contained herein. This does not affect your statutory rights.

This book contains passages which deal with racism, sexism, and gender issues, among other controversial topics.

About the Author

Jenny Harris is a researcher, writer and teacher living in Cambridge. She has recently completed a PhD at the University of Cambridge entitled 'Mirror, Fragment, Repetition: Using Metaphor to Read Twentieth-Century French Poetry in English Translation', which involved a lot of comparative close-reading.

She has taught English literature at the University of Cambridge and Anglia Ruskin University, as well as taking translation theory into schools as a Brilliant Club tutor. Her main claim to fame is having won University Challenge.

Rohan is the **Director of Operations** at *UniAdmissions* and is responsible for its technical and commercial arms. He graduated from Gonville and Caius College, Cambridge and is a fully qualified doctor. Over the last five years, he has tutored hundreds of successful Oxbridge and Medical applicants. He has also authored twenty books on admissions tests and interviews.

Rohan has taught physiology to undergraduates and interviewed medical school applicants for Cambridge. He has published research on bone physiology and writes education articles for the Independent and Huffington Post. In his spare time, Rohan enjoys playing the piano and table tennis.

The Ultimate English Literature Admissions Test Guide

Dr. Jenny Harris

Dr. Rohan Agarwal

UniAdmissions

Contents

The Basics 6

Preparing for the ELAT 12

Planning the Essay 14

Types of Comparison 19

Structuring your Response 21

Don'ts and Do's..23

Practice Papers...25

    Practice Paper A..25

    Practice Paper B 35

    Practice Paper C 43

    Practice Paper D..51

    Practice Paper E 60

Example Answers..67

    Practice Paper A..68

    Practice Paper B 78

    Practice Paper C 84

    Practice Paper D..89

    Practice Paper E 94

Reading List...103

Final Advice...106

Afterword 107

The Basics

What is the ELAT?

The ELAT is an exam, developed by Cambridge Assessment, to help Oxford and Cambridge universities to assess applicant to their English Literature courses at undergraduate level. The ELAT was introduced at Oxford in 2007, in 2018, the format of the ELAT changed slightly, so that only two rather than three of the texts are compared in the answer.

If you are applying to any of the following courses, you will need to sit the ELAT.

 English Literature at Oxford

 Classics and English at Oxford

 English and Modern Languages at Oxford

English Language and Literature at Cambridge

If you are applying to a joint honour course at Oxford, you will also need to take the CAT, the Classics Admissions Test, or the MLAT, Modern Language Admissions Test. Luckily, these are taken at interview, so you don't need to worry about trying to do two exams at once! If you are applying for History and English, you won't need to take the ELAT, but you will need to sit the History Admissions Test (HAT).

What does the ELAT consist of?

Section	Timing	FORMAT	Questions
ONE	90 Minutes	Essay	Compare two texts from six

Why is the ELAT used?

Oxford and Cambridge applicants tend to be a bright bunch and therefore usually have excellent grades. The vast majority of applicants score greater than 90% in all of their A level subjects, making it difficult to differentiate between them. This means that competition is fierce, so they use the ELAT to help differentiate between applicants who otherwise look similar on paper.

When do I sit ELAT?

The ELAT takes place alongside the other Oxbridge admissions tests at the end of \October or beginning of November each year. Dates vary slightly from year to year, so do check the Cambridge Assessment website to check.

Can I resit the ELAT?

No, you can only sit the ELAT once per admissions cycle.

Where do I sit the ELAT?

You can usually sit the ELAT at your school or college (ask your exams officer for more information). Alternatively, if your school isn't a registered test centre or you're not attending a school or college, you can sit the ELAT at an authorised test centre.

Do I have to resit the ELAT if I reapply?

If you reapply, you will have to resit the ELAT. This ensures that all applicants are being compared in a fair and equitable manner.

How is the ELAT Scored?

Each script is marked by two external examiners, each of whom gives the answer a mark out of thirty, These are combined to give an overall mark out of sixty. If there is a difference of five or more marks – for example a 22 from the first marker and 27 from the second, a third examiner marks the paper. The combined mark is then given as the sum of the two closest marks. If the third examiner gave the answer 29, then the combined score in our example would be 56.

How is the ELAT used?

Different Cambridge colleges will place different weightings on different components so it's important you find out as much information about how your marks will be used by emailing the college admissions office.

Oxford divides applicants into four bands based on the their marks:

Band 1: Likely to be interviewed (unless indication otherwise)

Band 2: Probably invited to interview

Band 3: May not be interviewed (unless indication otherwise)

Band 4: Unlikely to be interviewed (unless other factors outweigh the poor ELAT performance)

Cambridge don't use this banding system, and historically they have interviewed a higher proportion of applicants than Oxford.

As a guide, 66% of applicants to English Literature at Oxford in 2018 were shortlisted (which means invited to interview), and an even higher proportion for joint honours courses.

In general, the university will interview a high proportion of realistic applicants so the ELAT score isn't vital for making the interview shortlist. However, it can play a huge role in the final decision after your interview.

Getting a great score on the ELAT won't guarantee you a place or an interview, but your chances of being interviewed if you score in bottom few percentiles are slim.

How can I prepare for the ELAT?

This book is a great start! We've provided as much guidance as we can on how to write a university style response, rather than an A Level style one, which should help you take your writing to the level required for this exam.

In addition to this book, you can also use the Past Papers for the ELAT, which go all the way back to the first ELAT in 2007.

You can find these on the Cambridge Assessment website at: https://www.admissionstesting.org/for-test-takers/elat/preparing-for-elat/

The format of the exam changed in 2018, form comparing three extracts to two, so you can still use the older papers, but do keep in mind that the instructions will be a little out of date.

You'll also notice that some of the extracts in the Past Papers online are missing, as they are taken from works that are still under copyright. We've avoided this problem in our Mock Papers by only using sources that are no longer under copyright, but you should be aware that the real exam will feature more modern passages than these papers.

We chose to do this, as we felt that asking readers to purchase a book, only to discover that they needed to purchase further books or log onto websites to get the full value out of it was unfair, so we've made sure that all our Mock Papers are complete. This does mean that they don't perfectly reflect the ELAT that you'll sit, but they will still give you the practice you need.

However, we do also recommend practicing your comparison skills on more recent texts, so we've included a short reading list of texts we recommend for comparing alongside the passages we've chosen for our Mock Papers. We've tried to choose well known titles that are held by public libraries, are commonly available second hand or from charity shops, to ensure you can get hold of them easily.

In the case of poetry, you can find a huge quantity of modern poetry at the Poetry Foundation website, and we've made sure that as many of the poems as possible in our Reading List are available there for free.

Preparing for the ELAT

Before the exam

Read as widely as you can. The texts in the ELAT will be of different types (poetry, prose and drama) and can be from any period from Shakespeare onwards. The more widely and diversely you have read, the less likely you are to panic in the face of the texts on the exam.

Practise practise practise! You can use the specimen papers in this book and those on the Cambridge Assessment site to work on your techniques and timings as detailed below.

It will also be valuable to run practices of just the planning stage: pick two texts which are very different from each other and spend about half an hour making detailed notes on them and figuring out how you would make comparisons between them, and what kind of argument could be drawn out of these comparisons. The more easily you can get into a mindset of noticing interesting features and patterns in a text, and using them to think comparatively, the better.

And going back even further, you can also practice just the skimming and selection stage — take a past paper and time how quickly you can choose two texts.

In the exam

The exam is 90 minutes long, and the best way to use your time is to spend approximately 30 minutes reading and planning and 60 minutes writing.

You should skim all 6 texts as quickly as possible and commit firmly and early to your choice of which two to write about.

My advice is to choose your favourite text and pick one that looks like it might go with it. It might seem easier to compare two texts of the same kind — two extracts from novels, or two poems — or of a similar period or style.

The secret of comparison, though, is that almost any two texts can be productively compared! When learning to draw, it quickly becomes apparent that objects that seem 'simple' are in fact as rich in detail and difficulty as much more obviously complex ones. It is really a question of getting better at looking. The same is true of analysing texts. There is not really an 'easy' option, which is a daunting thought but also hopefully a liberating one.

If you like poems best, choose one or both poems. If novels are more your thing then that's a good choice for you. If there is a particular time period you feel most comfortable with, do select at least one text from this period if there is one, though be wary of the temptation to bring in outside material if it looks like texts you've seen before. Focus on the words on the page in front of you.

Choose as quickly as you can and try as hard as possible not to change your mind. Try not to panic, just keep paying close attention to the texts you have chosen and make notes, and some possible ways to compare them should become apparent.

Planning the Essay

Things to notice and compare

It is suggested in the rubric that you look at four aspects (well, actually it's five aspects but they've lumped two of them together):

Language

Imagery

Syntax

Form and Structure.

The Cambridge Assessment website adds 'allusion' to these, but an argument based on drawing out allusions to other texts from the texts given is likely not to do well based on the strong discouragement on the faculty websites from referring to outside material. If you can find a way to mention that the poem you've chosen alludes to Hamlet without referring to outside material (i.e. Hamlet), you should probably be applying for philosophy anyway!

It will be a good idea, and perhaps a good structuring principle for your essay, to try to hit all of these categories of analysis.

The thing about literary study that makes it distinct from other ways of reading texts (eg history) is a concern with the way the text creates ideas and meaning via its textuality, its words and sounds and rhythms and techniques and grammar and structure, which is to say, it is deeply concerned not so much with what a text means but how it means. This is what the list 'language, imagery, syntax, form and structure' is intended to remind you.

Firstly let us look at each of these things, and reflect on how it might be brought out in different kinds of text. This might form a kind of checklist to take with you into the 'reading and noticing' part of the test. Afterwards we will look at bringing texts of different kinds into conversation with each other.

A general pointer to bear in mind is that when analysing a text, you are attempting to spot when a pattern has been established and also when that pattern changes or is broken. This means you are analysing how the text progresses in a dynamic way, how it changes between the beginning and the end. This movement caused by the establishing and disrupting of patterns is what you need to compare between two texts, in which the types of pattern will be very different.

The list of categories of analysis is intended to help you spot patterns in the texts. When it comes to pattern spotting, there are no right and wrong answers, there is only material for which you can argue using evidence. Finding good evidence from inside the texts to support your points is the most crucial thing.

Form

What type of text is it?

Does it have a specific or traditional form? (such as a sonnet or novel)

How does the form relate to the content?

Structure

Units of meaning: paragraphs, stanzas, groups of lines: does the content of each paragraph or stanza change how you read the text?

Rhythm and metre: are there any moments in the text where the rhythm shifts? Why? NB prose can be rhythmic too, so this point is not only for poems which have a regular or familiar metre!

Rhyme: in a poem, is there rhyme? How does the rhyme structure change/contribute to the meaning?

Language

Techniques: what techniques are used? Why?

Tone: what is the tone of the text? Is it satirical? Melancholy? Romantic?

Style: what is the style of the language? Is it formal? Informal? Matter-of-fact? Lyrical?

Imagery

What images are used, if any?

Are they of a particular type?

What do the images used have in common? Do they change?

If there are no images, or fewer than you might expect, what effect does this have?

Syntax

How does the syntax (the way sentences/lines are structured grammatically) contribute to the meaning? Verbs, nouns, adjectives, conjunctions. Are there full stops? Commas? Dashes?

It is a really good idea to highlight or circle punctuation, and see if you can notice any patterns about how it is used to structure the text. Is the main unit the sentence, line, clause? Are they long or short?

Voice (who is speaking?)

Is it 1st or 3rd person?

 How many voices are there?

 How many 'presences' are there in the text? What are their roles?

 What is the tone of the voice?

Meaning

What is the obvious meaning?

Identify moments of change in the poem: what techniques create the change? What effect does this have on the meaning?

All the items in this list are useful when analysing and comparing any kinds of text, but since it is a feature of the ELAT to ask you to compare texts of different types, I will now include some specific pointers for comparing texts across genre and time.

Overall what you want to do is try to get a kind of 'map' of each text: where it starts, where it ends, what changes in between, and how that change is generated by shifts in language, imagery, syntax, form and structure. When you have maps of two texts you can put them side by side and see what important similarities and differences appear. Are they two very different texts that both end with a kind of punchline? Or contain a lot of description? Or use a central metaphor, or many different images?

It is also the case that all the texts in any one ELAT paper will be responding in different ways to a central theme. Although the ideas contained in a text are possibly less important for the ELAT than the way the text expresses them, you will want to have an interpretation of what those ideas are! This can then form a possible jumping-off point for your argument. Remember that the fact that the texts express different ideas is less interesting to your examiners than the differing ways those ideas are expressed, but drawing links between form and content is even better.

Types of Comparison

Poetry and Prose

The key when comparing poetry and prose is to remember that poetry can express complex ideas and narrative, and prose can use highly patterned language. Which is to say, the line between them is not as strict as you may have been led to believe. There is such a thing as a 'prose poem' after all! So, look for the 'poetic' features in the prose text: linguistic techniques of patterning and repetition could include use of punctuation, alliteration and rhyming, use of metaphor and simile,

And look for how the poem creates an argument, a story, a character, or a sense of place. See whether your two texts mainly structure themselves by long or short units (paragraphs, stanzas, couplets, clauses, single words).

Poetry and drama

The challenge when comparing a play text to another kind of text is that the techniques it has at its disposal to create meaning are quite specific: usually it can only use dialogue (or monologue) and stage directions which gesture towards a possible performance.

Drama is intended to be spoken aloud to an audience, but so are many poems. What aural effects can you find? Conversely, poetry often uses the space on the page in creative ways to contribute to structure and meaning. This may be in contrast to the ways a drama text might hint at use of the space of the stage.

What do the two texts do to create a sense of character or place, and to explore ideas?

Also, plays can be written in verse or in prose! If your play is in verse, you can use your regular poetry analysis techniques and compare how the poetry works in each text.

Prose and drama

Again, the unique features of drama (intended for performance, all dialogue,) will contrast with a prose extract. As you are comparing character or story or argument, never forget to focus on what the language does to create these effects.

Texts from Different Periods

When working with texts from very different periods, like when working with texts that are quite similar to each other, there can be a real temptation to dive into your contextual knowledge. Some elements of contextual knowledge, like recognising different verse forms (is this poem a sonnet or a villanelle? Or free verse?) could be very useful for analysis. However, it is mainly important to read each text very attentively and compare their linguistic features, without going too much into their differing contexts. Look for similarities in style, technique, imagery, narrative, even if they are used in very different ways, rather than going into detail about the differences which can simply be attributed to the difference in the time they were written.

Structuring your Response

The good news! This bit you (mostly) already know. The basics of essay structure do not change enormously between school and university level work, but you are expected to have internalised them really well, and at the same time a bit more freedom can be permitted in the service of an interesting point or argument.

However, when you are planning your ELAT answer you need to bear three things in mind:

1. DON'T discuss the passages one at a time — instead discuss them side by side in order to compare and contrast their features
2. DO try to give the two passages roughly equal attention
3. DO have a thread that brings your whole analysis together in the form of an argument

Introduction:

Start, fairly obviously, by saying which two texts you have chosen to compare. Since the brief for this essay is so incredibly wide, you will need to use the introduction to set out the basis of your comparison, and frame your argument.

Don't spend a whole paragraph summarising the texts for the sake of it: instead, if you choose to summarise, be very brief and make sure you use your summary to outline which aspects of the texts are actually relevant to your comparison. Your examiners are familiar with the texts, they want to know how you interpret them.

Body:

The body of the essay should consist of 2-4 paragraphs (long ones) in which you bring different aspects of your two texts into conversation with each other. Remember to try and hit the whole list of language, imagery, syntax, form and structure, though they will not all need their own paragraph.

Conclusion:

The conclusion is where you set out where your analysis of the two texts leaves your argument. What, in the final estimate, do they agree and differ on? Is there a particular feature of language, imagery, syntax, form or structure which draws them together (particularly if they seem very different) or sets them definitively apart (particularly if they appear more similar on the surface)?

Don'ts and Do's

DON'T:

Write too much! Three to four sides single spaced (about 750-900 words in most people's handwriting) is plenty. It is much more important to plan an argument and give good quality evidence from the texts than to write a really long essay. Sure a lucky few people can write superhumanly fast but if you find you're writing much more than 3-4 sides then try to spend more time on planning instead.

Bring in outside texts! There are no marks available for knowing a lot of contextual information about the texts or for comparing them to texts you know that are not on the paper. You might draw in a comment about the periods of the texts as a way to compare them but do not make a main point out of it. The aim is really to read the texts carefully and build your argument out of elements within them. If an extract is from a text you have read, you should avoid basing your essay on the text as a whole, but rather focus on the features of the passage in hand specifically.

DO:

Make an argument! The rubric of the test asks that you 'compare and contrast [two of the texts] in any ways that seem interesting to you'. A secret of Oxbridge essays is that even though they will not always explicitly ask for an argument, they ABSOLUTELY always want one. In your planning, when you have spent time with each text drawing out it's interesting features and contrasted them together, you then need to think of something that can be gained from reading these texts together, something that is made clearer, probably about the topic of the whole paper. This will be your argument. For example, in the paper on 'science', a comparison between two of the texts will probably draw out some different ways to think or write about science.

Have confidence! Go for the most interesting, sophisticated points you can, as long as you can find textual evidence for them. If inspiration strikes during the exam, go with it! Don't forget, the rubric asks you to compare in ways that seem interesting *to you*, and if you follow this advice and have a go at some practice papers, you definitely have grounds to believe in your ideas.

Practice Paper A

The following passages are all linked by the theme of science. They are arranged chronologically by date of publication. Read all the material carefully, and then complete the task below.

  A. From *An Anatomie of the World,* I. (1611), a poem by John Donne
  B. From *Natural Theology* (1805), a non-fiction text by William Paley
  C. From *Frankenstein* (1818), a novel by Mary Shelley
  D. *Sonnet – to Science* (1829), a poem by Edgar Allan Poe
  E. From *Hard Times* (1854), a novel by Charles Dickens
  F. *A Light Exists in Spring* (1896), a poem by Emily Dickinson

Select two of the passages (a) to (f) and compare and contrast them in any ways that seem interesting to you, paying particular attention to distinctive features of structure, language and style.

This task is designed to assess your responsiveness to unfamiliar literary material and your skills in close reading. Marks are not awarded for references to other texts or authors you have studied.

A. From *An Anatomie of the World*, I. (1611), a poem by John Donne

And new philosophy calls all in doubt,
The Element of fire is quite put out;
The Sun is lost, and th'earth, and no mans wit
Can well direct him where to look for it.
And freely men confesse that this world's spent,
When in the Planets, and the Firmament
They seeke so many new; and then see that this
Is crumbled out againe to his Atomies.
'Tis all in pieces, all cohaerence gone;
All just supply, and all Relation;
Prince, Subject, Father, Sonne, are things forgot,
For every man alone thinkes he hath got
To be a phoenix, and that then can bee
None of that kinde, of which he is, but hee.

B. From *Natural Theology* (1805), a non-fiction text by William Paley

IN crossing a heath, suppose I pitched my foot against a stone, and were asked how the stone came to be there; I might possibly answer, that, for any thing I knew to the contrary, it had lain there for ever: nor would it perhaps be very easy to show the absurdity of this answer. But suppose I had found a watch upon the ground, and it should be inquired how the watch happened to be in that place; I should hardly think of the answer which I had before given, that, for any thing I knew, the watch might have always been there. Yet why should not this answer serve for the watch as well as for the stone? why is it not as admissible in the second case, as in the first? For this reason, and for no other, viz.1 that, when we come to inspect the watch, we perceive (what we could not discover in the stone) that its several parts are framed and put together for a purpose, e.g. that they are so formed and adjusted as to produce motion, and that motion so regulated as to point out the hour of the day; that, if the different parts had been differently shaped from what they are, of a different size from what they are, or placed after any other manner, or in any other order, than that in which they are placed, either no motion at all would have been carried on in the machine, or none which would have answered the use that is now served by it. To reckon up a few of the plainest of these parts, and of their offices, all tending to one result:— We see a cylindrical box containing a coiled elastic spring, which, by its endeavour to relax itself, turns round the box. We next observe a flexible chain (artificially wrought for the sake of flexure), communicating the action of the spring from the box to the fusee.2 We then find a series of wheels, the teeth of which catch in, and apply to, each other, conducting the motion from the fusee to the balance, and from the balance to the pointer; and at the same time, by the size and shape of those wheels, so regulating that motion, as to terminate in causing an index3, by an equable and measured progression, to pass over a given space in a given time. We take notice that the wheels are made of brass in order to keep them from rust; the springs of steel, no other metal being so elastic; that over the face of the watch there is placed a glass, a material employed in no other part of the work, but in the room of which, if there had been any other than a transparent substance, the hour could not be seen without opening the case. This mechanism being observed (it requires indeed an examination of the instrument, and perhaps some previous knowledge of the subject, to perceive and understand it; but being once, as we have said, observed and understood), the inference, we think, is inevitable, that the watch must have had a maker: that there must have existed, at some time, and at some place or other, an artificer or artificers who formed it for the purpose which we find it actually to answer; who comprehended its construction, and designed its use.

C. From *Frankenstein* (1818), a novel by Mary Shelley

None but those who have experienced them can conceive of the enticements of science. In other studies you go as far as others have gone before you, and there is nothing more to know; but in a scientific pursuit there is continual food for discovery and wonder. A mind of moderate capacity which closely pursues one study must infallibly arrive at great proficiency in that study; and I, who continually sought the attainment of one object of pursuit and was solely wrapped up in this, improved so rapidly that at the end of two years I made some discoveries in the improvement of some chemical instruments, which procured me great esteem and admiration at the university. When I had arrived at this point and had become as well acquainted with the theory and practice of natural philosophy as depended on the lessons of any of the professors at Ingolstadt, my residence there being no longer conducive to my improvements, I thought of returning to my friends and my native town, when an incident happened that protracted my stay.

One of the phenomena which had peculiarly attracted my attention was the structure of the human frame, and, indeed, any animal endued with life. Whence, I often asked myself, did the principle of life proceed? It was a bold question, and one which has ever been considered as a mystery; yet with how many things are we upon the brink of becoming acquainted, if cowardice or carelessness did not restrain our inquiries. I revolved these circumstances in my mind and determined thenceforth to apply myself more particularly to those branches of natural philosophy which relate to physiology. Unless I had been animated by an almost supernatural enthusiasm, my application to this study would have been irksome and almost intolerable. To examine the causes of life, we must first have recourse to death. I became acquainted with the science of anatomy, but this was not sufficient; I must also observe the natural decay and corruption of the human body. In my education my father had taken the greatest precautions that my mind should be impressed with no supernatural horrors. I do not ever remember to have trembled at a tale of superstition or to have feared the apparition of a spirit. Darkness had no effect upon my fancy, and a churchyard was to me merely the receptacle of bodies deprived of life, which, from being the seat of beauty and strength, had become food for the worm. Now I was led to examine the cause and progress of this decay and forced to spend days and nights in vaults and charnel-houses. My attention was fixed upon every object the most insupportable to the delicacy of the human feelings. I saw how the fine form of man was degraded and wasted; I beheld the corruption of death succeed to the blooming cheek of life; I saw how the worm inherited the wonders of the eye and brain. I paused, examining and analysing all tthe minutiae of causation, as exemplified in the change from life to death, and death to life, until from the midst of this darkness a sudden light broke in upon me—a light so brilliant and wondrous, yet so simple, that while I became dizzy with the immensity of the prospect which it illustrated, I was surprised that among so many men of genius who had directed their inquiries towards the same science, that I alone should be reserved to discover so astonishing a secret.

D. *Sonnet – to Science* (1829), a poem by Edgar Allan Poe

Science! true daughter of Old Time thou art!
  Who alterest all things with thy peering eyes.
Why preyest thou thus upon the poet's heart,
  Vulture, whose wings are dull realities?
How should he love thee? or how deem thee wise,
  Who wouldst not leave him in his wandering
To seek for treasure in the jewelled skies,
  Albeit he soared with an undaunted wing?
Hast thou not dragged Diana from her car,
  And driven the Hamadryad* from the wood
To seek a shelter in some happier star?
  Hast thou not torn the Naiad* from her flood,
The Elfin from the green grass, and from me
The summer dream beneath the tamarind tree?
*Hamadryad; in Greek and Roman mythology, a nymph who lives in a tree and dies when the tree dies
*Naiad; in Greek and Roman mythology, a type of female spirit or nymph, presiding over bodies of fresh water

E. From *Hard Times* (1854), a novel by Charles Dickens

'You are to be in all things regulated and governed,' said the gentleman, 'by fact. We hope to have, before long, a board of fact, composed of commissioners of fact, who will force the people to be a people of fact, and of nothing but fact. You must discard the word Fancy altogether. You have nothing to do with it. You are not to have, in any object of use or ornament, what would be a contradiction in fact. You don't walk upon flowers in fact; you cannot be allowed to walk upon flowers in carpets. You don't find that foreign birds and butterflies come and perch upon your crockery; you cannot be permitted to paint foreign birds and butterflies upon your crockery. You never meet with quadrupeds going up and down walls; you must not have quadrupeds represented upon walls. You must use,' said the gentleman, 'for all these purposes, combinations and modifications (in primary colours) of mathematical figures which are susceptible of proof and demonstration. This is the new discovery. This is fact. This is taste.'

The girl curtseyed, and sat down. She was very young, and she looked as if she were frightened by the matter-of-fact prospect the world afforded.

'Now, if Mr. M'Choakumchild,' said the gentleman, 'will proceed to give his first lesson here, Mr. Gradgrind, I shall be happy, at your request, to observe his mode of procedure.'

Mr. Gradgrind was much obliged. 'Mr. M'Choakumchild, we only wait for you.'

So, Mr. M'Choakumchild began in his best manner. He and some one hundred and forty other schoolmasters, had been lately turned at the same time, in the same factory, on the same principles, like so many pianoforte legs. He had been put through an immense variety of paces, and had answered volumes of head-breaking questions. Orthography, etymology, syntax, and prosody, biography, astronomy, geography, and general cosmography, the sciences of compound proportion, algebra, land-surveying and levelling, vocal music, and drawing from models, were all at the ends of his ten chilled fingers. He had worked his stony way into Her Majesty's most Honourable Privy Council's Schedule B, and had taken the bloom off the higher branches of mathematics and physical science, French, German, Latin, and Greek. He knew all about all the Water Sheds of all the world (whatever they are), and all the histories of all the peoples, and all the names of all the rivers and mountains, and all the productions, manners, and customs of all the countries, and all their boundaries and bearings on the two and thirty points of the compass. Ah, rather overdone, M'Choakumchild. If he had only learnt a little less, how infinitely better he might have taught much more!

F. *A Light Exists in Spring* (1896), a poem by Emily Dickinson

A light exists in spring
Not present on the year
At any other period.
When March is scarcely here

A color stands abroad
On solitary hills
That science cannot overtake,
But human nature feels.

It waits upon the lawn;
It shows the furthest tree
Upon the furthest slope we know;
It almost speaks to me.

Then, as horizons step,
Or noons report away,
Without the formula of sound,
It passes, and we stay:

A quality of loss
Affecting our content,
As trade had suddenly encroached
Upon a sacrament.

Practice Paper B

The following passages are all linked by the idea of reflection. They are arranged chronologically by date of publication. Read all the material carefully, and then complete the task below.

- **A.** *Sonnet III* (1609) a poem by William Shakespeare
- **B.** *Nature* (1836), an extract from an essay by Ralph Waldo Emerson
- **C.** *A Hand-Mirror* (1848), a poem by Walt Whitman
- **D.** *Through the Looking Glass* (1871), an extract from the novel by Lewis Carroll
- **E.** *Passing and Glassing* (1906), a poem by Christina Rosseti
- **F.** *From Mrs Dalloway* (1925) a novel by Virginia Woolf

Select two of the passages (a) to (f) and compare and contrast them in any ways that seem interesting to you, paying particular attention to distinctive features of structure, language and style.

A. *Sonnet III* (1609) a poem by William Shakespeare

detatchment

Look in thy glass, and tell the face thou viewest
Now is the time that face should form another;
Whose fresh repair if now thou not renewest,
Thou dost beguile the world, unbless some mother,
For where is she so fair whose unear'd womb
Disdains the tillage of thy husbandry?
Or who is he so fond will be the tomb
Of his self-love, to stop posterity?
Thou art thy mother's glass, and she in thee
Calls back the lovely April of her prime:
So thou through windows of thine age shall see
Despite of wrinkles this thy golden time.
But if thou live, remember'd not to be,
Die single, and thine image dies with thee.

volta
line 8.

pinnacle
appearance

spring

ability to view

similarities with mother.

retain

duration

B. *Nature* (1836), an extract from an essay by Ralph Waldo Emerson

It has already been illustrated, that every natural process is a version of a moral sentence. The moral law lies at the centre of nature and radiates to the circumference. It is the pith and marrow of every substance, every relation, and every process. All things with which we deal, preach to us. What is a farm but a mute gospel? The chaff and the wheat, weeds and plants, blight, rain, insects, sun,—it is a sacred emblem from the first furrow of spring to the last stack which the snow of winter overtakes in the fields. But the sailor, the shepherd, the miner, the merchant, in their several resorts, have each an experience precisely parallel, and leading to the same conclusion: because all organizations are radically alike.

Nor can it be doubted that this moral sentiment which thus scents the air, grows in the grain, and impregnates the waters of the world, is caught by man and sinks into his soul. The moral influence of nature upon every individual is that amount of truth which it illustrates to him. Who can estimate this? Who can guess how much firmness the sea-beaten rock has taught the fisherman? how much tranquillity has been reflected to man from the azure sky, over whose unspotted deeps the winds forevermore drive flocks of stormy clouds, and leave no wrinkle or stain? how much industry and providence and affection we have caught from the pantomime of brutes? What a searching preacher of self-command is the varying phenomenon of Health!

C. *A Hand-Mirror* (1848), a poem by Walt Whitman

Hold it up sternly! See this it sends back! (Who is it? Is it you?)
Outside fair costume—within ashes and filth,
No more a flashing eye—no more a sonorous voice or springy step;
Now some slave's eye, voice, hands, step,
A drunkard's breath, unwholesome eater's face, venerealee's flesh,
Lungs rotting away piecemeal, stomach sour and cankerous,
Joints rheumatic, bowels clogged with abomination,
Blood circulating dark and poisonous streams,
Words babble, hearing and touch callous,
No brain, no heart left—no magnetism of sex;

Such, from one look in this looking-glass ere you go hence,
Such a result so soon—and from such a beginning!

D. Through the Looking Glass (1871), an extract from the novel by Lewis Carroll

'Now, if you'll only attend, Kitty, and not talk so much, I'll tell you all my ideas about Looking-glass House. First, there's the room you can see through the glass—that's just the same as our drawing room, only the things go the other way. I can see all of it when I get upon a chair—all but the bit behind the fireplace. Oh! I do so wish I could see that bit! I want so much to know whether they've a fire in the winter: you never can tell, you know, unless our fire smokes, and then smoke comes up in that room too—but that may be only pretence, just to make it look as if they had a fire. Well then, the books are something like our books, only the words go the wrong way; I know that, because I've held up one of our books to the glass, and then they hold up one in the other room.

'How would you like to live in Looking-glass House, Kitty? I wonder if they'd give you milk in there? Perhaps Looking-glass milk isn't good to drink—But oh, Kitty! Now we come to the passage. You can just see a little peep of the passage in Looking-glass House, if you leave the door of our drawing-room wide open: and it's very like our passage as far as you can see, only you know it may be quite different on beyond. Oh, Kitty! how nice it would be if we could only get through into Looking-glass House! I'm sure it's got, oh! such beautiful things in it! Let's pretend there's a way of getting through into it, somehow, Kitty. Let's pretend the glass has got all soft like gauze, so that we can get through. Why, it's turning into a sort of mist now, I declare! It'll be easy enough to get through—' She was up on the chimney-piece while she said this, though she hardly knew how she had got there. And certainly the glass was beginning to melt away, just like a bright silvery mist.

In another moment Alice was through the glass, and had jumped lightly down into the Looking-glass room. The very first thing she did was to look whether there was a fire in the fireplace, and she was quite pleased to find that there was a real one, blazing away as brightly as the one she had left behind. 'So I shall be as warm here as I was in the old room,' thought Alice: 'warmer, in fact, because there'll be no one here to scold me away from the fire. Oh, what fun it'll be, when they see me through the glass in here, and can't get at me!'

Then she began looking about, and noticed that what could be seen from the old room was quite common and uninteresting, but that all the rest was as different as possible. For instance, the pictures on the wall next to the fire seemed to be all alive, and the very clock on the chimney-piece (you know you can only see the back of it in the Looking-glass) had got the face of a little old man, and grinned at her.

'They don't keep this room so tidy as the other,' Alice thought to herself, as she noticed several of the chessmen down in the hearth among the cinders: but in another moment, with a little 'Oh!' of surprise, she was down on her hands and knees watching them. The chessmen were walking about, two and two!

E. Passing and Glassing (1906), a poem by Christina Rosseti

All things that pass
 Are woman's looking-glass;
They show her how her bloom must fade,
And she herself be laid
With withered roses in the shade;
 With withered roses and the fallen peach,
 Unlovely, out of reach
  Of summer joy that was.

 All things that pass
 Are woman's tiring-glass;
The faded lavender is sweet,
Sweet the dead violet
Culled and laid by and cared for yet;
 The dried-up violets and dried lavender
 Still sweet, may comfort her,
  Nor need she cry Alas!

 All things that pass
 Are wisdom's looking-glass;
Being full of hope and fear, and still
Brimful of good or ill,
According to our work and will;
 For there is nothing new beneath the sun;
 Our doings have been done,
  And that which shall be was.

F. From Mrs Dalloway (1925) a novel by Virginia Woolf

Laying her brooch on the table, she had a sudden spasm, as if, while she mused, the icy claws had had the chance to fix in her. She was not old yet. She had just broken into her fifty second year. Months and months of it were still untouched. June, July, August! Each still remained almost whole, and, as if to catch the falling drop, Clarissa (crossing to the dressing table) plunged into the very heart of the moment, transfixed it, there- the moment of this June morning on which was the pressure of all the other mornings, seeing the glass, the dressing table, and all the bottles afresh, collecting the whole of her at one point (as she looked into the glass), seeing the delicate pink face of the woman who was that very night to give a party; of Clarissa Dalloway; of herself.

perception from afar

How many millions of times had she seen her face, and always with the same imperceptible contraction! She pursed her lips when she looked in the glass. It was to give her face point. That was her self- pointed; dart-like; definite. That was her self when some effort, some call on her to be herself, drew the parts together, she alone knew how different, how incompatible and composed so for the world only into one center, one diamond, one woman who sat in her drawing room and made a meeting point, a radiancy no doubt in some dull lives, a refuge for the lonely to come to, perhaps; she had helped young people, who were grateful to her; she had tried to be the same always, never showing a sign of all the other sides of her- faults, jealousies, vanities, suspicions, like this of Lady Bruton not asking her to lunch; which, she thought (combing her hair finally), is utterly base! Now, where was her dress?

Practice Paper C

The following passages are all linked by the theme of dreams. They are arranged chronologically by date of publication. Read all the material carefully, and then complete the task below.

    A. From *Chaucer's Dream* (1597), an allegory attributed to Chaucer
    B. *The Dream* (1684), a poem by Aphra Behn
    C. An extract from *The Dream of a Ridiculous Man* (1877), a short story by Fyodor Dostoyevsky
    D. *We dream—it is good we are dreaming* (1890), a poem by Emily Dickinson
    E. *He Wishes for the Cloths of Heaven* (1899) a poem by WB Yeats
    F. From *Superstitions of the Highlands and Islands of Scotland, Collected entirely from Oral Sources* (1900) by John Gregorson Campbell

Select two of the passages (a) to (f) and compare and contrast them in any ways that seem interesting to you, paying particular attention to distinctive features of structure, language and style.

A. From *Chaucer's Dream* (1597), an allegory attributed to Chaucer

On a May night, the poet lay alone, thinking of his lady, and all her
beauty; and, falling asleep, he dreamed that he was in an island
Where wall, and gate, was all of glass,
And so was closed round about,
That leaveless none came in nor out; without permission
Uncouth and strange to behold;
For ev'ry gate, of fine gold,
A thousand fanes, ay turning, vanes, weathercocks
Entuned had, and birds singing contrived so as to emit
Diversely, on each fane a pair, a musical sound
With open mouth, against the air;
And of a suit were all the tow'rs, of the same plan
Subtilly carven aft flow'rs carved to represent
Of uncouth colours, during ay, lasting forever
That never be none seen in May,
With many a small turret high;
But man alive I could not sigh, see
Nor creatures, save ladies play, disporting themselves
Which were such of their array,
That, as me thought, of goodlihead for comeliness
They passed all, and womanhead.
For to behold them dance and sing,
It seemed like none earthly thing.

B. *The Dream* (1684), a poem by Aphra Behn

All trembling in my arms Aminta lay,
Defending of the bliss I strove to take;
Raising my rapture by her kind delay,
Her force so charming was and weak.
The soft resistance did betray the grant,
While I pressed on the heaven of my desires;
Her rising breasts with nimbler motions pant;
Her dying eyes assume new fires.
Now to the height of languishment she grows,
And still her looks new charms put on;
Now the last mystery of Love she knows,
We sigh, and kiss: I waked, and all was done.

'Twas but a dream, yet by my heart I knew,
Which still was panting, part of it was true:
Oh how I strove the rest to have believed;
Ashamed and angry to be undeceived!

C. An extract from *The Dream of a Ridiculous Man* (1877), a short story by Fyodor Dostoyevsky

Dreams, as we all know, are very queer things: some parts are presented with appalling vividness, with details worked up with the elaborate finish of jewellery, while others one gallops through, as it were, without noticing them at all, as, for instance, through space and time. Dreams seem to be spurred on not by reason but by desire, not by the head but by the heart, and yet what complicated tricks my reason has played sometimes in dreams, what utterly incomprehensible things happen to it! My brother died five years ago, for instance. I sometimes dream of him; he takes part in my affairs, we are very much interested, and yet all through my dream I quite know and remember that my brother is dead and buried. How is it that I am not surprised that, though he is dead, he is here beside me and working with me? Why is it that my reason fully accepts it? But enough. I will begin about my dream. Yes, I dreamed a dream, my dream of the third of November. They tease me now, telling me it was only a dream. But does it matter whether it was a dream or reality, if the dream made known to me the truth? If once one has recognised the truth and seen it, you know that it is the truth and that there is no other and there cannot be, whether you are asleep or awake. Let it be a dream, so be it, but that real life of which you make so much I had meant to extinguish by suicide, and my dream, my dream—oh, it revealed to me a different life, renewed, grand and full of power!

Listen.

I have mentioned that I dropped asleep unawares and even seemed to be still reflecting on the same subjects. I suddenly dreamt that I picked up the revolver and aimed it straight at my heart—my heart, and not my head; and I had determined beforehand to fire at my head, at my right temple. After aiming at my chest I waited a second or two, and suddenly my candle, my table, and the wall in front of me began moving and heaving. I made haste to pull the trigger.

In dreams you sometimes fall from a height, or are stabbed, or beaten, but you never feel pain unless, perhaps, you really bruise yourself against the bedstead, then you feel pain and almost always wake up from it. It was the same in my dream. I did not feel any pain, but it seemed as though with my shot everything within me was shaken and everything was suddenly dimmed, and it grew horribly black around me. I seemed to be blinded and benumbed, and I was lying on something hard, stretched on my back; I saw nothing, and could not make the slightest movement. People were walking and shouting around me, the captain bawled, the landlady shrieked—and suddenly another break and I was being carried in a closed coffin. And I felt how the coffin was shaking and reflected upon it, and for the first time the idea struck me that I was dead, utterly dead, I knew it and had no doubt of it, I could neither see nor move and yet I was feeling and reflecting. But I was soon reconciled to the position, and as one usually does in a dream, accepted the facts without disputing them.

D. *We dream—it is good we are dreaming* (1890), a poem by Emily Dickinson

We dream—it is good we are dreaming—
It would hurt us—were we awake—
But since it is playing—kill us,
And we are playing—shriek—

What harm? Men die—externally—
It is a truth—of Blood—
But we—are dying in Drama—
And Drama—is never dead—

Cautious—We jar each other—
And either—open the eyes—
Lest the Phantasm—prove the Mistake—
And the livid Surprise

Cool us to Shafts of Granite—
With just an Age—and Name—
And perhaps a phrase in Egyptian—
It's prudenter—to dream—

E. *He Wishes for the Cloths of Heaven* (1899) a poem by WB Yeats

HAD I the heavens' embroidered cloths,
Enwrought with golden and silver light,
The blue and the dim and the dark cloths
Of night and light and the half-light,
I would spread the cloths under your feet:
But I, being poor, have only my dreams;
I have spread my dreams under your feet;
Tread softly because you tread on my dreams.

F. From *Superstitions of the Highlands and Islands of Scotland*, Collected entirely from Oral Sources (1900) by John Gregorson Campbell

Dreams (Bruadar) have everywhere been laid hold of by superstition as indications of what is passing at a distance or of what is to occur, and, considering the vast numbers of dreams there are, it would be matter of surprise, if a sufficient number did not prove so like some remote or subsequent event, interesting to the dreamer, as to keep the belief alive. On a low calculation, a fourth of the population dream every night, and in the course of a year, the number of dreams in a district must be incredible. They are generally about things that have been, or are, causes of anxiety, or otherwise occupied men's waking thoughts. "A dream cometh through the multitude of business," Solomon says, and a Gaelic proverb says with equal truth "An old wife's dream is according to her inclination" (Aisling caillich mas a dùrachd). Its character can sometimes be traced directly to the health or position of the body, but in other cases, it seems to depend on the uncontrolled association of ideas. Out of the numberless phantasies that arise there must surely be many that the imagination can without violence convert into forebodings and premonitions. To dream of raw meat indicates impending trouble; eggs mean gossip and scandal; herring, snow; meal, earth; a grey horse, the sea. To dream of women is unlucky; and of the dead, that they are not at rest. In the Hebrides, a horse is supposed to have reference to the Clan Mac Leod. The surname of horses is Mac Leod, as the Coll bard said to the Skye bard:

"Often rode I with my bridle,/ The race you and your wife belong to."
In some districts horses meant the Macgnanean, and a white horse, a letter.

Practice Paper D

The following passages are all linked by the theme of water. They are arranged chronologically by date of publication. Read all the material carefully, and then complete the task below.

A. An extract from the play by William Shakespeare, *The Tempest* (1611)

B. An extract from book 1 of the epic poem by John Milton, *Paradise Lost* (1667)

C. A section from the poem by Tennyson Maud (1855)

D. A passage from the novel by George Eliot, *The Mill on the Floss* (1860)

E. An extract from the novel by Kate Chopin, *The Awakening* (1899)

F. An extract from the travel essay by Robert Louis Stevenson, *Alpine Diversions* (1905)

Task: Select two of the passages (a) to (f) and compare and contrast them in any ways that seem interesting to you, paying particular attention to distinctive features of structure, language and style.

A. An extract from the play by William Shakespeare, *The Tempest* (1611)

ARIEL. To every article.
  I boarded the King's ship; now on the beak,
  Now in the waist, the deck, in every cabin,
  I flam'd amazement. Sometime I'd divide,
  And burn in many places; on the topmast,
  The yards, and bowsprit, would I flame distinctly,
  Then meet and join Jove's lightning, the precursors
  O' th' dreadful thunder-claps, more momentary
  And sight-outrunning were not; the fire and cracks
  Of sulphurous roaring the most mighty Neptune
  Seem to besiege, and make his bold waves tremble,
  Yea, his dread trident shake.
PROSPERO. My brave spirit!
  Who was so firm, so constant, that this coil
  Would not infect his reason?
ARIEL. Not a soul
  But felt a fever of the mad, and play'd
  Some tricks of desperation. All but mariners
  Plung'd in the foaming brine, and quit the vessel,
  Then all afire with me; the King's son, Ferdinand,
  With hair up-staring-then like reeds, not hair-
  Was the first man that leapt; cried 'Hell is empty,
  And all the devils are here.'

B. An extract from book 1 of the epic poem by John Milton, *Paradise Lost* (1667)

He scarce had ceased when the superior Fiend
Was moving toward the shore; his ponderous shield,
Ethereal temper, massy, large, and round,
Behind him cast. The broad circumference
Hung on his shoulders like the moon, whose orb
Through optic glass the Tuscan artist views
At evening, from the top of Fesole,
Or in Valdarno, to descry new lands,
Rivers, or mountains, in her spotty globe.
His spear—to equal which the tallest pine
Hewn on Norwegian hills, to be the mast
Of some great ammiral, were but a wand—
He walked with, to support uneasy steps
Over the burning marl, not like those steps
On Heaven's azure; and the torrid clime
Smote on him sore besides, vaulted with fire.
Nathless he so endured, till on the beach
Of that inflamed sea he stood, and called
His legions—Angel Forms, who lay entranced
Thick as autumnal leaves that strow the brooks
In Vallombrosa, where th' Etrurian shades
High over-arched embower; or scattered sedge
Afloat, when with fierce winds Orion armed
Hath vexed the Red-Sea coast, whose waves o'erthrew
Busiris and his Memphian chivalry,
While with perfidious hatred they pursued
The sojourners of Goshen, who beheld
From the safe shore their floating carcases
And broken chariot-wheels. So thick bestrown,
Abject and lost, lay these, covering the flood,
Under amazement of their hideous change.

C. A section from the poem by Tennyson Maud (1855)

Is that enchanted moan only the swell
Of the long waves that roll in yonder bay?
And hark the clock within, the silver knell
Of twelve sweet hours that past in bridal white,
And died to live, long as my pulses play;
But now by this my love has closed her sight
And given false death her hand, and stol'n away
To dreamful wastes where footless fancies dwell
Among the fragments of the golden day.
May nothing there her maiden grace affright!
Dear heart, I feel with thee the drowsy spell.
My bride to be, my evermore delight,
My own heart's heart and ownest own farewell;
It is but for a little space I go:
And ye meanwhile far over moor and fell
Beat to the noiseless music of the night!
Has our whole earth gone nearer to the glow
Of your soft splendours that you look so bright?
I have climb'd nearer out of lonely Hell.
Beat, happy stars, timing with things below,
Beat with my heart more blest than heart can tell,
Blest, but for some dark undercurrent woe
That seems to draw—but it shall not be so:
Let all be well, be well.

D. A passage from the novel by George Eliot, *The Mill on the Floss* (1860)

At that moment Maggie felt a startling sensation of sudden cold about her knees and feet; it was water flowing under her. She started up; the stream was flowing under the door that led into the passage. She was not bewildered for an instant; she knew it was the flood!
The tumult of emotion she had been enduring for the last twelve hours seemed to have left a great calm in her; without screaming, she hurried with the candle upstairs to Bob Jakin's bedroom. The door was ajar; she went in and shook him by the shoulder.

"Bob, the flood is come! it is in the house; let us see if we can make the boats safe."

She lighted his candle, while the poor wife, snatching up her baby, burst into screams; and then she hurried down again to see if the waters were rising fast. There was a step down into the room at the door leading from the staircase; she saw that the water was already on a level with the step. While she was looking, something came with a tremendous crash against the window, and sent the leaded panes and the old wooden framework inward in shivers, the water pouring in after it.

"It is the boat!" cried Maggie. "Bob, come down to get the boats!"

And without a moment's shudder of fear, she plunged through the water, which was rising fast to her knees, and by the glimmering light of the candle she had left on the stairs, she mounted on to the window-sill, and crept into the boat, which was left with the prow lodging and protruding through the window. Bob was not long after her, hurrying without shoes or stockings, but with the lanthorn in his hand.

"Why, they're both here,—both the boats," said Bob, as he got into the one where Maggie was. "It's wonderful this fastening isn't broke too, as well as the mooring."

In the excitement of getting into the other boat, unfastening it, and mastering an oar, Bob was not struck with the danger Maggie incurred. We are not apt to fear for the fearless, when we are companions in their danger, and Bob's mind was absorbed in possible expedients for the safety of the helpless indoors. The fact that Maggie had been up, had waked him, and had taken the lead in activity, gave Bob a vague impression of her as one who would help to protect, not need to be protected. She too had got possession of an oar, and had pushed off, so as to release the boat from the overhanging window-frame.
"The water's rising so fast," said Bob, "I doubt it'll be in at the chambers before long,—th' house is so low. I've more mind to get Prissy and the child and the mother into the boat, if I could, and trusten to the water,— for th' old house is none so safe. And if I let go the boat—but you," he exclaimed, suddenly lifting the light of his lanthorn on Maggie, as she stood in the rain with the oar in her hand and her black hair streaming.

Maggie had no time to answer, for a new tidal current swept along the line of the houses, and drove both the boats out on to the wide water, with a force that carried them far past the meeting current of the river.

In the first moments Maggie felt nothing, thought of nothing, but that she had suddenly passed away from that life which she had been dreading; it was the transition of death, without its agony,—and she was alone in the darkness with God.

E. An extract from the novel by Kate Chopin, *The Awakening* (1899)

The water of the Gulf stretched out before her, gleaming with the million lights of the sun. The voice of the sea is seductive, never ceasing, whispering, clamoring, murmuring, inviting the soul to wander in abysses of solitude. All along the white beach, up and down, there was no living thing in sight. A bird with a broken wing was beating the air above, reeling, fluttering, circling disabled down, down to the water.

Edna had found her old bathing suit still hanging, faded, upon its accustomed peg.

She put it on, leaving her clothing in the bath-house. But when she was there beside the sea, absolutely alone, she cast the unpleasant, pricking garments from her, and for the first time in her life she stood naked in the open air, at the mercy of the sun, the breeze that beat upon her, and the waves that invited her.

rebirth, cleansing

How strange and awful it seemed to stand naked under the sky! how delicious! She felt like some new-born creature, opening its eyes in a familiar world that it had never known.

The foamy wavelets curled up to her white feet, and coiled like serpents about her ankles. She walked out. The water was chill, but she walked on. The water was deep, but she lifted her white body and reached out with a long, sweeping stroke. The touch of the sea is sensuous, enfolding the body in its soft, close embrace.

intimacy

She went on and on. She remembered the night she swam far out, and recalled the terror that seized her at the fear of being unable to regain the shore. She did not look back now, but went on and on, thinking of the blue-grass meadow that she had traversed when a little child, believing that it had no beginning and no end.

Her arms and legs were growing tired.

She thought of Leonce and the children. They were a part of her life. But they need not have thought that they could possess her, body and soul. How Mademoiselle Reisz would have laughed, perhaps sneered, if she knew! "And you call yourself an artist! What pretensions, Madame! The artist must possess the courageous soul that dares and defies."

Exhaustion was pressing upon and overpowering her.
"Good-by—because I love you." He did not know; he did not understand. He would never understand. Perhaps Doctor Mandelet would have understood if she had seen him—but it was too late; the shore was far behind her, and her strength was gone.

She looked into the distance, and the old terror flamed up for an instant, then sank again. Edna heard her father's voice and her sister Margaret's. She heard the barking of an old dog that was chained to the sycamore tree. The spurs of the cavalry officer clanged as he walked across the porch. There was the hum of bees, and the musky odor of pinks filled the air.

detachment

F. An extract from the travel essay by Robert Louis Stevenson, *Alpine Diversions* (1905)

There is all manner of variety in the nature of the tracks, some miles in length, others but a few yards, and yet like some short rivers, furious in their brevity. All degrees of skill and courage and taste may be suited in your neighbourhood. But perhaps the true way to toboggan is alone and at night. First comes the tedious climb, dragging your instrument behind you. Next a long breathing-space, alone with snow and pine-woods, cold, silent, and solemn to the heart. Then you push off; the toboggan fetches away; she begins to feel the hill, to glide, to swim, to gallop. In a breath you are out from under the pine-trees, and a whole heavenful of stars reels and flashes overhead. Then comes a vicious effort; for by this time your wooden steed is speeding like the wind, and you are spinning round a corner, and the whole glittering valley and all the lights in all the great hotels lie for a moment at your feet; and the next you are racing once more in the shadow of the night with close-shut teeth and beating heart. Yet a little while and you will be landed on the high-road by the door of your own hotel. This, in an atmosphere tingling with forty degrees of frost, in a night made luminous with stars and snow, and girt with strange white mountains, teaches the pulse an unaccustomed tune and adds a new excitement to the life of man upon his planet.

Practice Paper E

The following passages are all linked by the theme of rain. They are arranged chronologically by the date of publication. Read all the material carefully, and then complete the task below.

- **A.** Extract from *Il Mystico* (1862), a poem by Gerard Manley Hopkins
- **B.** From *Wuthering Heights* (1847), a novel by Emily Brontë
- **C.** From *Frankenstein*, (1818) a novel by Mary Shelley
- **D.** Act 4, Scene 1, *The Merchant of Venice* a play by William Shakespeare
- **E.** From *The Great Gatsby*, a novel by F. Scott Fitzgerald
- **F.** From *The Hound of the Baskervilles*, a novel by Sir Arthur Conan Doyle

Select two of the passages (a) to (f) and compare and contrast them in any ways that seem interesting to you, paying particular attention to distinctive features of structure, language and style.

A. Extract from *Il Mystico* (1862), a poem by Gerard Manley Hopkins

To hear his strain descend less loud
On to ledges of grey cloud;
And fainter, finer, trickle far
To where the listening uplands are;
To pause — then from his gurgling bill
Let the warbled sweetness rill,
And down the welkin, gushing free,
Hark the molten melody;
In fits of music till sunset
Starting the silver rivulet;
Sweetly then and of free act
To quench the fine-drawn cataract;
And in the dews beside his nest
To cool his plumy throbbing breast.
Or, if a sudden silver shower
Has drench'd the molten sunset hour,
And with weeping cloud is spread
All the welkin overhead,
Save where the unvexed west
Lies divinely still, at rest,
Where liquid heaven sapphire-pale
Does into amber splendours fail,
And fretted clouds with burnish'd rim,
Phoebus' loosen'd tresses, swim;
While the sun streams forth amain
On the tumblings of the rain,
When his mellow smile he sees
Caught on the dark-ytressed trees,
When the rainbow arching high
Looks from the zenith round the sky,
Lit with exquisite tints seven
Caught from angels' wings in heaven,

Double, and higher than his wont,
The wrought rim of heaven's font, —
Then may I upwards gaze and see
The deepening intensity
Of the air-blended diadem,
All a sevenfold-single gem,
Each hue so rarely wrought that where
It melts, new lights arise as fair,
Sapphire, jacinth, chrysolite,
The rim with ruby fringes dight,
Ending in sweet uncertainty
'Twixt real hue and phantasy.

B. From *Wuthering Heights* (1847), a novel by Emily Brontë

The following evening was very wet: indeed, it poured down till day-dawn; and, as I took my morning walk round the house, I observed the master's window swinging open, and the rain driving straight in. He cannot be in bed, I thought: those showers would drench him through. He must either be up or out. But I'll make no more ado, I'll go boldly and look.' Having succeeded in obtaining entrance with another key, I ran to unclose the panels, for the chamber was vacant; quickly pushing them aside, I peeped in. Mr. Heathcliff was there—laid on his back. His eyes met mine so keen and fierce, I started; and then he seemed to smile. I could not think him dead: but his face and throat were washed with rain; the bed-clothes dripped, and he was perfectly still. The lattice, flapping to and fro, had grazed one hand that rested on the sill; no blood trickled from the broken skin, and when I put my fingers to it, I could doubt no more: he was dead and stark!

C. From *Frankenstein*, (1818) a novel by Mary Shelley

Morning, dismal and wet, at length dawned and discovered to my sleepless and aching eyes the church of Ingolstadt, its white steeple and clock, which indicated the sixth hour. The porter opened the gates of the court, which had that night been my asylum, and I issued into the streets, pacing them with quick steps, as if I sought to avoid the wretch whom I feared every turning of the street would present to my view. I did not dare return to the apartment which I inhabited, but felt impelled to hurry on, although drenched by the rain which poured from a black and comfortless sky.

D. Act 4, Scene 1, *The Merchant of Venice* a play by William Shakespeare

The quality of mercy is not strained;
It droppeth as the gentle rain from heaven
Upon the place beneath. It is twice blest;
It blesseth him that gives and him that takes:
'T is mightiest in the mightiest; it becomes
The throned monarch better than his crown:
His sceptre shows the force of temporal power,
The attribute to awe and majesty,
Wherein doth sit the dread and fear of kings;
But mercy is above this sceptred sway;
It is enthronèd in the hearts of kings,
It is an attribute to God himself;
And earthly power doth then show likest God's
When mercy seasons justice. Therefore, Jew,
Though justice be thy plea, consider this,
That, in the course of justice, none of us
Should see salvation: we do pray for mercy;
And that same prayer doth teach us all to render
The deeds of mercy. I have spoke thus much
To mitigate the justice of thy plea;
Which if thou follow, this strict court of Venice
Must needs give sentence 'gainst the merchant there.

E. From *The Great Gatsby*, a novel by F. Scott Fitzgerald

About five o'clock our procession of three cars reached the cemetery and stopped in a thick drizzle beside the gate—first a motor hearse, horribly black and wet, then Mr. Gatz and the minister and I in the limousine, and, a little later, four or five servants and the postman from West Egg in Gatsby's station wagon, all wet to the skin.

As we started through the gate into the cemetery I heard a car stop and then the sound of someone splashing after us over the soggy ground. I looked around. It was the man with owl-eyed glasses whom I had found marvelling over Gatsby's books in the library one night three months before. I'd never seen him since then. I don't know how he knew about the funeral or even his name. The rain poured down his thick glasses and he took them off and wiped them to see the protecting canvas unrolled from Gatsby's grave. I tried to think about Gatsby then for a moment but he was already too far away and I could only remember, without resentment, that Daisy hadn't sent a message or a flower.

Dimly I heard someone murmur 'Blessed are the dead that the rain falls on,' and then the owl-eyed man said 'Amen to that,' in a brave voice. We straggled down quickly through the rain to the cars. Owl-Eyes spoke to me by the gate. 'I couldn't get to the house,' he remarked. 'Neither could anybody else.' 'Go on!' He started. 'Why, my God! they used to go there by the hundreds.' He took off his glasses and wiped them again outside and in.

F. From *The Hound of the Baskervilles*, a novel by Sir Arthur Conan Doyle

October 17th. — All day to-day the rain poured down, rustling on the ivy and dripping from the eaves. I thought of the convict out upon the bleak, cold, shelterless moor. Poor devil! Whatever his crimes, he has suffered something to atone for them. And then I thought of that other one — the face in the cab, the figure against the moon. Was he also out in that deluged — the unseen watcher, the man of darkness? In the evening I put on my waterproof and I walked far upon the sodden moor, full of dark imaginings, the rain beating upon my face and the wind whistling about my ears. God help those who wander into the great mire now, for even the firm uplands are becoming a morass. I found the black tor upon which I had seen the solitary watcher, and from its craggy summit I looked out myself across the melancholy downs. Rain squalls drifted across their russet face, and the heavy, slate-coloured clouds hung low over the landscape, trailing in gray wreaths down the sides of the fantastic hills. In the distant hollow on the left, half hidden by the mist, the two thin towers of Baskerville Hall rose above the trees. They were the only signs of human life which I could see, save only those prehistoric huts which lay thickly upon the slopes of the hills. Nowhere was there any trace of that lonely man whom I had seen on the same spot two nights before.

Example Answers

These answers were written under exam conditions by UniAdmissions tutors, none of whom have studied English Literature at degree level, but did study it at A level. This should mean that they represent an accurate picture of what a typical applicant's answer would look like, rather than a perfect answer written by an English PhD student.

They are each accompanied by examiner's comments, in italics, as well as a formal mark. These were marked by a former ELAT marker at Cambridge, so they should be an accurate representation of the kind of feedback and scoring that would occur in the real exam.

We recommend that you attempt each practice question yourself before turning to these answers, as practicing approaching the extract blind is among the most important parts of your preparation.

While not all possible pairings of extracts have been treated in these answers – that would have meant seventy five mock answers for just five papers! – we have tried to make sure that these answers give a broad range of ideas for possible responses, as well as analyses of their strengths and weaknesses.

Practice Paper A

Passages A&B

There are several interesting comparisons that can be made between two texts: 'An Anatomie of the World', which is a poem written by renowned writer, John Donne and 'Natural Theology', a non-fiction text written by William Paley. Paley was best known from this wonrk, whereby he submits an exposition, outlining the teleological argument, which outlines the existence of God based on intelligent design in the natural world. Donne, on the other hand, was a clergyman who was well known for his sermons and his spiritual works. Both these writers integrate their prior vast knowledge of religion and spirituality in order to convey their true meaning to the reader.

Uses contextual knowledge of the writers, which is not necessary. Does well to set up an argument based on the way the writers each use religion.

In 'Natural Theology' by Paley, he argues that there has to be a scope for the existence of a higher being, such as a God, due to the fact that everything in the natural world is designed with such intelligence and genius that it, in fact, cannot be a result of luck and fortune, as per the Big Bang Theory. Paley writes about the intricacies that are required to design something as detailed as the natural world by comparing it to the technicalities of a watch. He discusses all the various factors that make up a common watch, something that it is not given much of a second look. His frighteningly accurate description of a watch and its function is impressive to say the least. Paley's use of language to describe the 'cylindrical box containing a coiled elastic spring' and his meticulous detail cleverly draws a comparison to the complexities of nature.

This paragraph needs more textual evidence. 'Frighteningly accurate description' - why? What is frightening here? There is only one quotation at the end of the paragraph to illustrate the point about Paley's exhaustive detail, it is well-chosen but there should be more. What is it about Paley's language that makes a sense of great detail and how does it support his point?

On the other hand, in Donne's 'An Anatomie of the World', the poet uses the idea of a higher being in order to highlight the lost nature of free will that man possesses, and how often the elements and a higher being are the ones that ultimately control one's decisions and conclusions. The title itself 'An Anatomie of the World' shows how Donne believes that the world is structured. He truly envisages the natural world being created by the 'Father'. He has put 'man' on the earth to think with what he has been given.

What is it precisely that the word 'Anatomie' in the title suggests about Donne's view of the structure of the world? This paragraph misunderstands the poem somewhat, as it is not 'free will' that is lost but rather the worldview that puts the earth at the centre of the universe rather than the sun. It is true that Donne's poem suggests belief in a creator God, but how does he use language, imagery, structure to do this? And what is the poem arguing?

Structurally, these works are strikingly different. On the one hand, you have a poem by Donne, briefly underlying the anatomy of the natural world and how he believes the earth functions, with use of the elements and free will. On the other, you are presented with an extract from a larger work. Paley uses analogical examples to convey a similar message as Donne has done. His more detailed analysis of a watch attempts to describe the similarities when it comes to the convolutions of nature.

'Analogical' is a good word in an otherwise rather incoherent paragraph. Paley's text is structured in part by numerical lists. It would have been worth mentioning that here. Also although it is difficult, a more detailed account of Donne's poem's structure would definitely be helpful.

The key underlying theme in both of these works is the idea or notion of religion, and how the natural world came to be. In conclusion, both these texts attempt to convey that similar notion through different mediums.

Paley successfully shows his thoughts and ideas through a comparison of the complexity of a watch to nature. Donne, on the other hand, takes a different approach using the medium of poem to deconstruct nature, if you will, by outlining the composition of the natural world, and how it uses various ways to come together. This is through the use of the elements and the introduction of man.

Interesting observation that the texts are conveying 'a similar notion'. The idea that there is some threat to the religiously ordained order of the world is common to both texts, but Paley's response is to defend creationism, whereas Donne seems to use cosmic imagery to argue that human beings have lost a sense of certainty about their place in the world, and to lament this. All in all, this essay contains some accurate analysis but does not develop a reading of Donne's poem and needs to go much deeper into thinking about language, imagery, form and structure as it makes its argument.

Numerical mark: 17/30

Passages C&D

The authors of the two passages present distinct relationships between notions of 'science' and 'art'. Both play on the validity of this dichotomy in their texts.

A good start which clearly and briefly sets out the parameters of the argument.

Poe takes great pains to imbue his work with a sense of the importance of a Western 'art' tradition. His obedience to traditional Petrarchan sonnet form and the smattering of self-important ancient Greek references show that he prides and is trying to emulate this classical past. In his mind, the ultimate sin of science is its removal of the mystery of life and, in effect, the mystery of religion, a task that was once reserved for the pulpit. Science is a "Vulture" that "preyest upon the Poet's heart", "whose wings are dull realities". He perceives science as a block to slowly revealing and experiencing the beauty of creation. Science's aim, in his mind, is to pick the bones clean; a poet's is to fill it with life. In his view, the poet is a warrior-explorer, besieged by the attempt to know and reveal all about the world. The poet is almost an innocent, seeking "for treasure in the jeweled skies" and soaring "with an undaunted wing" despite his many attacks. Poe is drawing on a rich semantic field of aerial metaphors to give his poet a sense of purpose and lofty ambition. Here the American poet is tapping into both Romantic and Classical notions of science. On the one hand, his protagonist is a clear conduit for Romantic notions of heroism in art, yet the Classical dichotomy between the two fields of knowledge is clearly present.

Very good to point out the traditional sonnet form. What is it about the Greek references that comes across as 'self-important'? Good analysis of Poe's use of language, backed up with appropriate quotations.

This confusion, of whether to present the artist figure as victim or victor, leads us to a picture of Poe as saccharine and navel-gazing. He seems confused as to whether he articulates the voices of the ancients or his own personal opinion, as epitomized in the victim persona he inhabits "beneath the Tamarind tree". This is a black and white view of the possibilities (or restrictions, as Poe would have you believe) of 'science', contrasted with the full, elaborate classical world under attack. The specific classical figures which he mentions hover between tangible reality and symbolism, as if Poe imagines that they are both a real and imaginary foe of the "Vulture". This self-consciousness, both of his own place within the history of art and poetry, and of his position as a poet, is typical of the style that emerged amongst poets of the time. The firm classical foundations of European politics that had been smashed by the Napoleonic wars revealed a group of rulers governed by self-interest and 'disaster management', rather than any code of honour. America's role within this was even more complex, as a side player. The art of the emerging United States was saturated in the values of republicanism and other 18th century failed projects. America found itself clutching after a dead set of values by which to define their own.

Two paragraphs is too long to write about only one text: they need to be brought into conversation with one another. The analysis is good but the historical context, while accurate, is not really necessary and takes the essay a bit too far away from analysing the texts in question.

Shelley, on the other hand, sees no opposition between the worlds of 'art' and science', and revels in the quivering line between the two. Frankenstein is a Byronic scientist and Shelley paints us a picture of a man obsessed by his 'art'. As in Poe's work, our protagonist is presented as aloof: "None but those who have experienced them can conceive of the enticements of science." Our initial impression is of a self-important, unreliable narrator whose story we can trust as little as Poe's. Yet the novel format allows for a psychological exploration of a clash between 'science' and 'art'. The chunky paragraphs give us a significant opportunity to understand this man so beholden to an art that is abstract to most readers, and Shelley takes us through science's particular attractions. In Shelley's view, science is a combination of examining "the cause and progress" and "supernatural enthusiasm", of anatomy and inspiration. In this personality, Shelley (like Poe) incorporates both Romantic and Classical notions of the relationship between science and art. Frankenstein embraces a poetic, personal approach to science, yet it is underlined by the implication of scientists as consumers of life, of seekers of "food for discovery and wonder". But unlike Poe, Shelley reveals this tension implicitly and through the reader's extensive engagement with Frankenstein and the progress of the plot. Where Shelley's text is a multilayered exploration, Poe's is a cursory sketch.

Again, what is it about Shelley's use of language and structure that causes the narrator to seem 'self-important' and 'unreliable'? Slightly too much of this paragraph is paraphrase. '(like Poe)' in parentheses is not sufficient to compare and contrast the texts, though the point is good. The point about consumption/eating is very well-observed but would be better made in a separate paragraph that introduced both Poe's vulture and Shelley's 'food for discovery' side by side. Can you give a specific example of Shelley revealing tension 'implicitly'?

However, it is only Frankenstein's actions that mark him out as 'mad, bad and dangerous to know'. What makes him captivating as a character is the flat, almost scientific, way in which he describes his experiments and achievements. The final sentence of the first paragraph is long, interrupted only by a few commas to help the reader catch their breath. Effectively Frankenstein is claiming his academic supremacy over Ingolstadt's staff, yet the reader can imagine it delivered in a flat, almost careless tone. Whereas Poe wallows in the abstraction of classical references, Shelley mostly writes with a deadpan style, first and foremost to imbue the account with a sense of scientific realism. This is partly an inheritance of an epistolary tradition from the previous century, and employs some of the sensationalist characteristics of that genre to hold the reader's interest. Samuel Richardson used the same technique to explore the moral complexities of marriage in 'Pamela'. But as well as offering a flat canvas through which to explore the many dimensions of a monolithic 'science', the canvas is there for us to put ourselves in Frankenstein's shoes. The age of alchemy and discovery had expired in the previous century, and the scientific theories that came to dominate the intellectual scene of the early 19th century (such as those promoted by Erasmus Darwin) were embedded in ideas of the everyman and of reform. Whereas Poe considers scientists as all-powerful demolishers of culture, Shelley frames them as closer to us than we would believe.

Good analysis of syntax. How is Shelley's 'deadpan' style created? Comparison to Samuel Richardson cannot be given any credit as it refers to an outside text. Mentioning that it is in an epistolary form is and describing its effect on this text specifically is all that is required. All comparisons should be between Shelley and Poe! Again the emphasis on historical context is interesting but not within the remit of this test.

An interesting example of this is the religious tone that Shelley adopts at the end of the extract. The "light so brilliant and wondrous, yet so simple" is almost prophetic in tone, as if Frankenstein's moment of genius is a gift from God rather than his own volition. This presentation of scientific genius as akin to divine inspiration seems to be rooted in the Methodist traditions of John Wesley, and marks Frankenstein as both defying God and inspired by his divine maker. Poe sees science as an affront to God and poets (both of whom are revellers of "treasure in the jewelled skies"), simultaneously masking and laying bare the mysteries of the universe. But Shelley seems to conceive of religion and science as two sides of the same coin.

There is a lot about this essay which is very good indeed, but unfortunately it makes the mistake of treating the texts too much one at a time rather than drawing them together. Ideally every paragraph would refer to both texts and draw them together thematically and technically. There is also too much context and reference to outside texts. Where it does draw direct comparisons between the texts it is very strong indeed and the use of textual evidence to support points is excellent.

Numerical mark: 23/30

Passages E&F

This answer compares and contrasts passages from Charles Dickens and Emily Dickinson, in respect to matters of interest, structure, language, and style.

Dickens, or rather his characters, present an objective view of the world, whilst Dickinson explores her personal, and therefore subjective, experiences of the natural world which the scientific method is unable to either quantify or qualify. There is a sterility to Dickens' prose which is diametrically opposed to Dickinson's passionate account. That is not to say that Dickens' passage is not loquacious. The gentleman within the passage takes great care to elucidate the desired extent of regulation and governmentality of his institution, and this is mirrored in the list of academic paraphernalia within which Mr. M'Choakumchild has been immersed. The narrator reflects upon these diatribes, with humour, but only once they have been thoroughly notated. Thus, the 'scientific method' is allowed full explanation, but Dickens ensures his own view (that reducing the complexity of the world to singular truths does not do Being justice) swiftly follows.

I am not sure about the use of 'objective' here - does it mean 'third-person' or is it in reference to the obsession with 'facts'? The accusation of 'sterility' misses the humour in Dickens' descriptions. It is good to point out that the Dickens passage does also include direct authorial commentary. Slightly more Dickinson in this paragraph would give it more balance.

Structurally, the passages are starkly different. Within Dickens' text, the vast majority of narrative is dedicated to exploring numerous objective observances. It is only in the final sentence that the narrative bubble is abruptly burst, and Dickens offers his own view of the foolishness of the gentleman in the story. Meanwhile, Dickinson's passage has an organic flow. A romantic exposition of the beauty of the light which exists in spring slowly manifests into something more melancholic. Therefore, whilst the mood of both texts drastically change, this happens suddenly within Dickens' passage whilst Dickinson's mood changes are more consistent, and always subtle. The macrostructures, and the reasoning behind them, is mirrored within the microstructures of the text. For example, the list of disciplines which Mr M'Choakumchild is acquainted ("orthography, etymology, syntax, and prosody, biography, astronomy, geography, and general cosmography, the sciences of compound proportion, algebra, land-surveying and levelling, vocal music, and drawing from models") begins with something which is both quantifiable and qualifiable, but finishes with pure art. Thus, the disciplines have been ranked according to their position of dominance within hierarchies of academia, but only tacitly. The opening line of Dickinson's poem ("A light exists in spring") is a direct replication of the title. Her changes of mood are subtle, and this is heightened once the reader has acquired the false sense of security offered by the grounded title and opening line.

This paragraph is a good example of putting the texts side by side and contrasting them. Good use of textual evidence to show how the textual effects are created.

Both Dickens and Dickinson's use of language serve the aims of their texts. The characters in Dickens' passage either use short sentences comprised of short words ("This is the new discovery. This is fact. This is taste.") to prove that complex phenomena can be reduced to simplified notions of truth, or are composed of long lists of words with Latin derivations ("orthography, etymology, syntax, and prosody, biography, astronomy, geography, and general cosmography etc") to prove the profundity of experience which can be derived from knowledge. All of the words (and all of the lines) are relatively short within Dickinson's poem. Thus, the reader is not distracted by changes of language, but is relaxed into her phenomenological account.

Again a good contrast is made between the stylistic elements of each text.

There is an absence of nature in Dickens' account - references to features of engineering, such as the "pianoforte", are prioritised over explorations of the natural world. Dickinson's poem exists as a phenomenological interrogation of the natural world. She invites the reader to connect with the light of spring through other senses. For example, hearing: "It almost speaks to me". Furthermore, the Spring scene is personified ("A color stands abroad / On solitary hills"), and thus the reader engages in a mental conversation with their surroundings. The reader is given an account of the physical world, invited into the 'imaginary' world, which is then personified, and thus allowed to develop their own feelings through conversation with the personified landscape. When Dickens references distance, it is through disciplines of scientific observation such as astronomy or cosmology, but Dickinson continually references distance to direct the reader through her imaginary landscape. For example, "It shows the furthest tree", "Upon the furthest slope we know", "It passes, and we stay", and "As trade had suddenly encroached".

Good to see more close-reading of Dickinson here. Quotations used well to illustrate points.

Ultimately, both Dickens and Dickinson believe that the scientific method is useful, but is not an omniscient phenomena as of itself. Dickens allows the objective method to be elucidated, before damning the approach in one final sentence. Dickinson revels in the unquantifiable nature of Being, and her use of the word "sacrament" with its religious connotations as her final offering is testament to this.

This essay has really got the hang of getting both texts in each paragraph to compare and contrast them. Some of the claims about Dickens early on are a bit difficult to substantiate ('sterile' language) and it misses some of the humorous tone, and slightly more focus on Dickinson might have been welcome but it is a good attempt and one which comes to a conclusion well.

Numerical mark: 21/30

Practice Paper B

Passages D&E

Both Lewis Carroll in Passage D and Christina Rossetti in Passage E are concerned with changes of state. Where Christina Rossetti explores the changes made by time, portraying worldly things as reassuringly temporary, Carroll playfully undermines the supposed solidity of reality by attesting to the power of imagination, in creating new worlds that stretch beyond the set passage of time.

Good introduction which brings the texts together and forms an argument out of what they have in common.

Rossetti establishes temporality through imagery of touch. The crackling 'withered roses', representing the 'woman' aging, vividly mimic the frailty of aged skin and the sharpness of bone tangible through it, creating a potent sensual reminder of the inescapability of this change of state. However, Rossetti also evokes the 'dried lavender / Still sweet', combining the image of dryness once again with an olfactory image of the 'sweet' scent of lavender. Rossetti enhances this additional image of a dead plant in order to show that despite the inescapability of aging and time, sweetness and enjoyment is still possible. She emphasises this with a last tactile image of heat, 'there is nothing new beneath the sun'. The warmth of the 'sun' can be both brutal and comforting; in this contradiction, Rossetti communicates to the reader that acknowledging the temporariness of life is both lamentable and a form of calming release.

It would be better to refer to both texts in each paragraph. However this is a good example of close-reading Rosetti's imagery.

Carroll's exploration of a change of state, although far more fantastical than Rossetti's, similarly focuses on tactile imagery. At the simple proposition of Alice, 'Let's pretend the glass has got all soft like gauze,' the mirror starts to 'melt away', and is then described as a 'mist'. Alice is able to make the solidity of the 'glass' go through the chemical changes of state, solid 'soft like gauze', then liquid 'melt[ing]', then the gas of a 'mist', solely through use of 'pretend[ing]' and her imagination. The ease with which Alice's childlike imagination can change the certainties of physics shows Carroll is happily disregarding the same inevitabilities of existence that Rossetti thoughtfully embraces. In this world of the imagination, the 'clock on the chimney-piece', the embodiment of the passage of time, now has 'the face of a little old man'. Carroll twists the concerns that Rossetti explores, regarding the inescapable submission of human beings to time, by changing the state of time itself. He fuses it with a 'grinn[ing]' human face, suggesting that time itself has now been impishly bested by human imagination. Through the Looking-Glass, the novel from which the extract is sourced, is a children's book: Carroll could well be demonstrating to his young intended audience that maintaining one's imaginative faculties frees oneself from the constraints of aging.

Good use of quotation here, and good discussion of imagery, and this paragraph keeps the thread of the argument going as well as being more comparative, going between the two texts.

Rossetti, on the other hand, suggests freedom from the constraints of aging can only be gained in acceptance of it. Each octave of her poem employs the rhyme scheme of a couplet, 'pass / glass' a triplet, 'fade / laid / shade', another couplet, 'peach / reach', and then an irregular rhyme to end each stanza, 'was / [...] Alas! [...] was', a rhyme repeated in the final line of all three stanzas. The pattern of couplet-triplet-couplet builds a cyclical rhythm in each stanza, which is always gently interrupted by the irregular rhyme in each final line. Rossetti's choice of structure reflects the inevitable pattern of aging, building to and decreasing from a climax, and reaching a sudden, albeit gently repeated, stop. Carroll's use of free indirect discourse in his narrative, by contrast, emphasises the power of Alice through her dialogue. Her speech is what enables her to imagine herself out of the strictures of narrative and into a new existence. 'Oh, what fun it'll be, when they see me through the glass in here, and can't get at me!' Carroll re-emphasises the power created by imagination to break through patterns of inevitability through portraying Alice as gleefully asserting her independence through dialogue, a dominant figure against time in her new, created world.

Good comparisons of the way each text uses language, which also advances the argument.

Overall, both Carroll and Rossetti explore changes of state for different ends. Rossetti urges an embrace of the rhythm of life, and emphasises there is still 'sweet[ness]' to be found in aging. Carroll, on the other hand, proposes the inevitability of aging can be playfully demolished through use of one's imagination.

Conclusion does well to draw the two texts together, though it would be even better if there were a sentence on how each text uses mirrors specifically to talk about aging. This is a very good response which combines sophisticated analysis of each text with apposite comparisons and develops an argument.

Numerical mark: 25/30

Passages A&F

Shakespeare in Passage A and Woolf in Passage F both discuss the concept of self-reflection, analysing oneself retrospectively. Whilst Shakespeare makes this discussion to encourage readers to change how they present themselves, Woolf's work relates to concealment of the true self from others.

The sonnet seems to me to have a specific addressee rather than the general reader. But this introduction sets up the parameters for comparison well.

Both writers discuss the concept of self-reflection by referencing mirrors. Intriguing, both writers create this imagery by using the metaphor of glass to portray a mirror. This could be argued to be a product of the historical context. Shakespeare's sonnet was completed in 1609, so perhaps a "look in thy glass" was a synonym for observing oneself in the mirror in that era. However, since Woolf chooses the same descriptor of having "looked into the glass" in the more modern times of 1925, perhaps the use of this literary device is more intentional. The effect of the writers referring to mirrors as glass may be to mislead readers into thinking literal glass, such as a window, is being referred to. Later context then makes it apparent that this interpretation was incorrect. For example, in Woolf's passage the first reference to glass is followed up with descriptions of "the dressing table, and all the bottles afresh", making it clear the glass being referred to must instead be a mirror on a dressing table. Likewise, Shakespeare's reference to glass precedes what "thou viewest", revealing that something can be seen in the glass and it is therefore reflective and so it must instead be a mirror that is being referred to. The act of misleading the reader to make an incorrect interpretation, then supplying them with context to go back and correct this judgement, means the reader is forced to reflect upon their understanding of the writing and change their prior conceptions. The fact that this process occurs at the beginning of both pieces of writing means that from the offset of the works the reader is being made to personally reflect upon their judgements and understanding. This means the theme of reflection is not only present literarily in the passages, but also physically in the reader by making them interact with the passages in a reflective way through the use of ambiguity. Both writers therefore convey the theme of reflection by instilling it early within the reader themselves. This sets the tone for the self-reflection related commentary that the rest of the passage discusses, meaning it is more likely that these messages will be engaged with and understood by the reader.

The point about ambiguity within the texts causing the reader to 'reflect' is very good, even though the specific example of ambiguity chosen probably only applies to a modern reader ('glass' as a synonym for mirror is common in both Shakespeare and Woolf's times)

Since the remainder of both texts discusses how the writers view themselves, it is particularly important to have the readers reflect upon their own self judgements using the glass ambiguity technique to make these discussions even more emotionally relevant and salient to the reader. Both texts discuss the writers' views of themselves in the context of how others may see them. In Shakespeare's sonnet, the writer reveals how if one does not share their life with others they will "die single, and thine image dies with thee". This reveals to the reader that if they do not express who they truly are to others by living a single life, then they will take that secret about their true self to the grave. This appears to be a warning to the reader, due to the use of morbid imagery related to death. Moreover, the sonnet is structured so that this is the last line the reader interacts with, meaning that it sticks with them as the take home message from the sonnet to share their image of themselves with others to avoid their image of themself dying alone. Furthermore, the syllable structure of the sonnet shortens from eleven to ten syllables as the sonnet progresses. This loss of content from the sonnet as it progresses reflects the loss of interaction and engagement Shakespeare is suggesting the reader may have if they do not share their image with others. Woolf, however, conveys a different message, as the writer promotes instead hiding who one really is from others namely "never showing a sign of all the other sides of her- faults, jealousies, vanities, suspicions". Whilst the mirror in Woolf's passage is "collecting the whole of her at one point", the character reveals how what the mirror reflects about themselves is not what the character reveals to others about themselves as they instead hide negative aspects of themselves to others. Therefore, whilst Shakespeare's sonnet tells a story of how one's "face should form another" impression of oneself in the mirror to portray to others who they reveal are, Woolf instead appears to appeal to secrecy. Accordingly, Woolf's passage ends with "Now, where was her dress?". This abrupt interruption to the writer's train of thought that was reflecting on how they hide their true character, shows that rather than now changing their outward projection of themselves they are instead going to repress their doubts and continue to hide their true reflection of themselves even more, which is confirmed with this final imagery relating to the character seeking further disguise in the form of the costume of a dress.

It is not correct to say that the texts discuss 'how the writers view themselves' - Mrs Dalloway is a fictional novel, and in this passage a character is looking at herself in the mirror and the reader is given access to her thoughts via a technique called 'stream of consciousness'. Meanwhile, the lyric 'I' in Shakespeare's sonnets also cannot be automatically presumed to correspond to the thoughts of the writer, it also constructs a character. Again, the sonnet is addressed to 'thou' which is not the reader but rather another character.

Shakespeare and Woolf therefore use the same ambiguity technique to instill a reflective attitude in the readers in order to make them more deeply engage with their different styles of thought about self-reflection. This is because whilst Shakespeare encourages the reader to make their self-reflection match up more closely with the story about themselves that they tell others, Woolf portrays how the whole self that the mirror reveals is something that might continue to be hidden from others.

Fictional and poetic texts should not be read simply as trying to send a 'message' to the reader or give advice. It is interesting to engage with the reader's possible responses to a text (for example in the first paragraph the ambiguity of the texts might correspond to a reader's needing to reflect more), however a close reading of the texts themselves must be concerned with how they are structured and how they use language and imagery and how they 'work', on their own terms and in relation to one another.

Numerical mark: 13/30

Practice Paper C

Passages A&E

In passage A, Chaucer's Dream, the poet describes the dream he had after admiring and fantasising about the beauty of his lady. His dream follows a similar theme of wonder and charm as he describes the atmosphere of his surroundings, the architecture of concrete objects and buildings, and the scene of alluring ladies rejoicing.

In passage E, He Wishes for the Cloths of Heaven, the poet describes a longing to provide an array of cloths, extravagant and lavish in nature. But he cannot do so, being poor and can only dream of said act. The poet does not characterise the individual for whom he wishes to give his desired wealth to, but one can imagine that this would be someone near and dear to him, perhaps a lady unsurprisingly. To compensate for the lack of treasure and affluence, he presents the entirety of his being and what one can presume is his aspiration/ambition to become something better, to the subject of his dreams.

Both passages describe dreams in an imaginative and utopian manner, and they both involve an additional character that the poets fancy or have a deep fondness of. Both poets also included the characterisation of colours in their narrative to emphasise their message. However, the content of both passages are distinctive and highly divergent from each other: passage A merely outlines the scenic ambience of his surroundings influenced by his love for his lady, whilst passage E depicts a deep-rooted sense of longing.

The language and style of passage E is more contemporary in nature compared to passage A as the former features a simpler structure/prose with a straightforward meaning whilst the latter gives prominence to more medieval, elaborate metaphors, rendering it harder to comprehend. Passage A is also more descriptive and enlightening, giving the reader a vivid illustration of the poet's dreams. In contrast, passage E leaves more room for imagination and interpretation in terms of what the poet meant by 'dreams'. Passage E portrays a stronger emotion of vulnerability and authenticity interwoven with somber tones, whereas there is a sense of lightness and superficiality in passage A without delving much into the mental state of the poet. Passage E is structured in a form that is more rhythmic, with a repeating and consistent pattern. On the other hand, passage A varies to a larger extent in terms of structure from one sentence to another.

This essay is a bit short to meet the criteria for an answer. The first two paragraphs, which are made up of summaries of the two passages, fail to set up the terms of an argument, though they are accurate. The third paragraph, which constitutes the comparison, contains some interesting ideas but they are not sufficiently backed up with evidence from the texts, and very few quotations are used.

Numerical mark: 12/30

Passages C&F

Both Dostoyevsky and Campbell texts, explore the intrinsic nature of dreams and its particular significance to reality. Each author however, leads the reader to a different conclusion-whereas Dostoyevsky, through his passage expresses the incomprehensible and impenetrable nature of dreams and their deep connection to reality, Campbell, through a informative and detached approach presents evidence to suggest that dreams are both superstitious and attached to local cultures, rather than truly reflective of reality.

Slightly incoherent first sentence but this introduction does a very good job of introducing an argument via brief summaries of the pertinent aspects of the two texts.

Dostoyevsky´s extract, like Campbell´s begins with a firm assertion about dreams. The former, begins by inviting the reader to reflect upon the variety of possible ways in which one may experience a dream. Unlike

Campbell, throughout his text he penetrates the innermost psychological and physical experience of dreams. Campbell, on the other hand, speaks about dreams as an outsider, from the perspective of an investigator.

A quotation of the 'firm assertions' would have been very helpful here, but a useful comparison is drawn and the texts are effectively placed in conversation with one another.

Dostoyevsky's stream of consciousness mirrors the lack of clarity experienced in dreams. His initial informative tone and assertions regarding dreams exposes his ability to theoretically conceptualise dreams. This is soon juxtaposed by inability to comprehend his own dreams. The juxtaposition between the theoretical clarity but emotional confusion is mirrored by the structure of the initial sentences: the anaphora Dreams, introduce assertively factual information about them (for instance about how they may be experienced and where they come from), whilst the following remark "yet" indicate his inability to apply these facts to his own dreams. This confusion is further mirrored through the rhetorical questions in which he asks himself how his reasoning is not being questioned when he is interacting with his dead brother in his dream This state of perplexion culminates at the end, when, although the reader knows that he is dreaming, he adopts a strongly authoritative tone when asserting that he: "was dead, utterly dead, [he] knew it and had no doubt of it". Campbell, conversely, does not let go of his authority and confidence in the information he is presenting to the reader. The repetition of number and informative lexis, such as calculation and a fourth, assert the truth in the evidence is providing. His external and de-focalised examination of dreams (looking at general trends the whole population) invites the reader to rationalise the emotional experience of dreams. Whereas Dostoyevsky, as we shall see, uses this perplexion to express the emotive nature of dreams which is later confirmed through the clear presence of suicidal emotions both in the world of dreams and reality, Campbell uses the lack of emotion as a rhetorical device to establish his reliability. Instead, numbers and logic provide evidence that mathematical chance makes it necessary for events, people and objects of our dreams to overlap with our reality.

Some really good analysis of form and structure here, and the essay continues to put the two texts side by side. Again a little more quotation might provide stronger evidence for the points.

Not only does Dostoyevsky display confusion, throughout the passage he is also clearly experiencing deep emotions. For instance, the passage often jumps from long and slow sentences to short and sharp ones, as the author is attempting to direct his line of thought. A notable instance of this comes after the rather long rhetorical questions, when he is reminiscing about his experiences with his dead brother in his dreams, which are then suddenly contrasted with "but enough" as the author attempts to limit indulging in these emotive thoughts. The clear emotional attachment of his dead brother, gives his following description of suicidal thoughts a source. This is symbolised by the scenario of suicide which he had reasoned for in real life, in which he shoots his head, with the suicidal scenario in his dream, in which he redirects the gun to his heart, to show the reader that the emotional pain is present in both. There is an undeniable link between his pain in dreams and in life. The expression of these emotions is therefore key in convincing the reader between them and the events of his dreams.

Campbell's main tool is not emotion, but rather authority in convincing the reader that the connections between reality and dreams are insignificant. Although this is mainly achieved through his authoritative tone, the inclusion of a long list of apparent symbolic meanings of dreams reduces the significance of each of them, especially since the lack of information gives the impression that they are completely abstract. Finally, the reference to specific clans and social groups which are highly localised, gives the reader an example of localised and superstitious beliefs, which undermine their potential to express universal truth.

Again the comparisons are well-drawn. A concluding sentence to sum up the argument would have been nice to have and a little more quotation from Campbell would make the points about that text a little clearer, but this is overall a very good answer.

Numerical mark: 23/30

Practice Paper D

Passages C&E

Both Maud by Tennyson and The Awakening by Chopin use water, specifically the sea, as a medium in their texts through which other experiences are possible. In both texts, there is a heavy use of the sea as an evoker of memory - though neither text limits those evocations to the sea itself.

A good initial comparison setting up the theme of the argument as the sea

Each text, relatively early on, makes reference to the sound of the sea. Chopin is heavier in her use of personification, describing its "voice" as "seductive, never ceasing, whispering, clamoring, murmuring" - giving it an intentionality that Tennyson's initial description of the sea lacks. There is almost a suggestion that it is possible to be in conversation with Chopin's sea, whereas Tennyson only specifies an "enchanted moan" is heard.

Very good focus on linguistic techniques and drawing the two texts together

Tennyson, however, does recreate the sound of the sea throughout his poem using the poem's structure. It is - excepting the last line - written in iambic pentameter with almost no deviations. Lines end in one of four possible rhymes, with B lines appearing only near the first half of the poem, and D lines only in the second half. B lines seem connected to the real, physical world, whereas D lines tend to refer to the narrator's constructed reality. A and C lines are present in all sections of the poem. There is no clear organised distribution for the rhymes, nor are there any verse breaks; instead lines are woven with each other, which may replicate the motion of waves on a shore.

Interesting interpretation and good, focused close-reading of the structure of the poem

Chopin is more explicit in her description of the setting, providing readers with details such as scale and colour "all along the white beach", whereas Tennyson's narrator is not. Chopin is keen for readers to link Edna's situation with a more general experience of the sea, and how it can interact with people. The sea is described in present tense, allowing readers to compare it with their own experience. Edna's personal interaction with the sea is in past tense, however we are invited to take it as an example of a potentially universal experience. Chopin also uses the injured bird, "circling disabled down", to foreshadow Edna's experience later in the passage.

Again good discussion of techniques and use of quotation to support the points being made

For Tennyson, however, little attention is paid to real-world surroundings. His "enchanted moan" is not necessarily only the sea; it is also a sound that wells up from his memory. The name "Maud" is only mentioned in the title, however the poem itself seems to be about the narrator's memory of her. The sound of the sea triggers a chain of memories - "the clock within" that, rather than chronological time, is more concerned with the narrator's recollection of Maud.

Tennyson's narrator seems to hold little melancholy in these memories. Maud "died to live, long as my pulses play". Death is not, for the narrator, an end; it is called a "false death", perhaps because the narrator's memories - aided by the sea - are sufficiently vivid for the narrator to resurrect her in his mind. The narrator is aware that his mind is not occupying reality, calling these recollections "footless fantasies", with alliteration used to emphasise their artificial nature. Maud - who is addressed directly later in the poem - is said to "beat to the noiseless music of the night". The use of an oxymoron "noiseless music" indicates that the narrator is both aware of, and accepting of, this unreality. The imagined landscape is described as "dreamful wastes", though with little negative connotations; instead, it is as being the home of his "evermore delight".

Edna, in Chopin's text, also finds memories triggered by the sea. She is reminded of a previous night when she "swam far out" and had a "fear of being unable to regain the shore". Like Tennyson's narrator, Edna compares a memory with her current situation - but Tennyson's poem emphasises and favours the memory. Edna's fearful memory is sidelined in favour of a more decisive present, whereas Tennyson's narrator envelops his present self in a memory - but both characters are the happier for it.

As each character delves further into the water - literally for Edna, metaphorically for Tennyson's narrator - each seems to experience a sense of vindication.

Again, this is a good place to draw the two texts together and make a direct comparison, one which serves to advance the argument

Edna displays a sense of defiance, when discussing Leonce and her children: "they need not have thought that they could possess her, body and soul". Though it is not explicit in the passage, it is implied that Edna is rejecting their assumption by wading into the Gulf. A similarly defiant attitude is shown to Mademoiselle Reisz. Little explanation is given for why Edna wishes to defy their expectations - but her determination is clear; she continues until "exhaustion".

Tennyson's narrator seems to entrench himself further into his imagination, and gives readers reasons for doing so. The dreamlike reality is populated with Maud's "soft splendours", and is linked to light and brightness. This is contrasted with a "lonely Hell" - presumably the narrator's reality after Maud's real-world death. Lines 20 and 21 begin with an imperative "Beat", as the stars are linked with the narrator's "blest" heart, with "blest" being repeated in line 22. The sea's ability to augment Tennyson's narrator's unreality is described in a positive light.

For Chopin's Edna, the sea's ability to emphasise a memory is less unambiguously positive. She too is linking the location with being able to commune with persons not present, such as Doctor Mandelet, though her words "Good-by – because I love you" are not explicitly optimistic. The text refers to a missed opportunity - some meeting with Doctor Mandelet which may have altered Edna's course - though the specifics are not shown to be relevant.

Excellent use of quotation to provide evidence for points which advance the argument

In the final paragraph, Edna seems to enter an unreality that Tennyson's narrator entered significantly earlier in the text. Edna's memory of her "old terror" vanishes as quickly as it appears, to be replaced with other memories. Crucially, at this point in the text, verbal phrases such as "remembered", "thinking of", and "thought of" are lost. Instead, verbs such as "heard" are used. Chopin states that "[t]here was the hum of bees, and the musky odor of pinks" - an assertion rather than an evocation. We cannot be certain of Edna's attitude towards this entry into unreality - though some acceptance or welcoming is implied, as no terror is present. Whether Edna dies in this text is unclear - though, as with Tennyson's narrator - it may be that death is not an ending in this constructed reality.

Tennyson's narrator also suppresses less savoury aspects of his memories, referencing them only as "some dark undercurrent". This is one of the only instances in the later section of the poem where water itself is used as an image, perhaps because the narrator is sufficiently embedded in his memory for any water - physical or not - to be ignorable. Tennyson's poem, too, ends with an assertion: the undercurrent "shall not" draw. His recreation of a time with Maud is strong enough for this to be defeated. The poem ends with a short, repetitive exhortation: "let all be well, be well", indicating a peace the narrator has found in his memory.

Neither text seems to be particularly preoccupied with drawing the reader into either character's specific memory, and little is specified about the seascape in either text. This lack of specificity is shared by water in general; it is one of the few items universal to all human experience. The underspecificity of both descriptions in terms of imagery allows each reader to construct their own setting in which the respective passages take place. This will inherently be connected to a reader's own experiences and memories. Underspecification can make the central idea of each text - that the sea can help people evoke, enhance, and inhabit a coherent set of memories - easier for any given reader to attempt to replicate.

Some very good comparisons and excellent close-reading and analysis of imagery, form and structure. The arguments arise directly out of the points of comparison between the texts, truly bringing them into conversation with one another and generating interpretations which are interesting and original. The focus is entirely on these two texts and the ways they can be compared, without bringing in a lot of context or any outside texts.

Numerical mark: 28/30

Practice Paper E

Passages A&C

In both passages A and C, rain provides an atmospheric backdrop to the main events taking place or being described. Although rain is not explicitly the subject of either, it colours our perception of the escape from the monster (as in Frankenstein), and provides a framework with which to interpret the song of the bird, and to appreciate the beauty of the rainbow referenced in the poem.

Good opening which sets out parameters for comparison

In the poem, rain is integrated seamlessly into the description of the birdsong. The first two lines evoke the image of a divine origin for both the song and the rain as they 'descend' from what must be heaven, onto 'ledges of grey cloud'. Although in the first stanza, only birdsong is mentioned explicitly, the use of language that could apply equally to song and to rain, creates the effect of inextricably intertwining music and rain. The allusions to music and liquids further this effect: 'gurgling' is a bubbling sound, created by the rapid movement and frothing of water - creating ambiguity as to whether birdsong or rain is being referenced. The movement of water is also used to describe the song of the bird, and this attributes a flowing yet firmly physical quality to it. The 'warbled sweetness' 'gushing free' evokes an image of a thirst-quenching mountain brook; almost playful. The 'melody' is referred to as 'molten' - a more obvious stating of the comparisons between rain and song, and similarly, the sense of relief that water brings is similar to how the bird 'quenches' and refreshes the stale atmosphere.

The passage is different to the poem in this respect. The rain takes more of a background role in the events, and serves to heighten the feelings of apprehension experienced by the character and communicated to the reader. Rain is only mentioned twice in the passage, heading and ending the passage. This indicates that although the rain at most provides an atmospheric background to the events, it plays an subtler yet fairly important role in colouring the reader's misgivings. This is in stark contrast to the poem, where the ambiguity and confusion created when the writer uses language that applies equally to the rain and birdsong explicitly intertwines the two.

Nice comparison and great use of examples to show how the poem interweaves the sounds of the rain and the birdsong.

An insight into the role played by the theme of rain in both passages can be gained from examining movement and pace. The poem has the rhyming scheme AABBCC, etc. which gives a strong sense of fast-paced movement, almost a gallop. This is in keeping with the allusions to flow, rhythm and the development of musical phrases. There is a sense of playful, benign action, similar to listening to the warbling, changing progression of a birdsong. In Frankenstein, the sense of movement that is communicated to the reader is rather different. Anxious verbs such as 'pacing', 'hurry', 'sought' pepper the passage, and is, as a result, pervaded by a feeling of fear. There is also a marked sense of the situation slipping out of control. The character does not take decisive action to accelerate his pace, but feels instead 'impelled' to do so, and the unfavourable weather acts upon him, rather than existing merely as a background. The morning 'dawned' and is 'discovered to' him, giving a sense that he is at the mercy of the elements. Inevitability is a powerful tool here, and is used to heighten the sense of foreboding. The poem, meanwhile, is firmly centred in 'his nest' (the nest of the songbird), despite meandering in imagery in a playful way.

A very good paragraph bringing together detailed close-reading of both texts, particularly their structure and style

In addition to the effects it has on the other events in the poem and in the passage, certain connotations are ascribed to the rain. The poem describes several, varying interpretations of the effects of rain, and the rain takes on different qualities as the poem continues, whereas the passage presents only one. After comparing rain and birdsong in the first stanza, the second stanza takes on a slightly darker tone. The first word, 'or' indicates to the reader that an alternative perception of rain is to be given. A silver shower is 'sudden', and 'drench'd' the 'molten sunset hour', which prescribes remarkably antagonistic qualities to the rain. It is almost as if a battle is being waged between the hot colours of the sunset (this quality furthered by the adjective 'molten' which prescribes a lava-like, liquid-metal-like quality to the evening) and the cooling rain. The cloud is 'weeping' – a forceful adjective that connotes an extreme, almost hysterical sadness. In addition to this, the clouds are 'fretted', and the rain falls as 'tumblings'. These descriptions describe the rain as being wildly emotional, and out of control, in particular 'tumbling' evokes the imagery of the rain falling in a disorderly, chaotic fashion. This particular description is reminiscent of the atmosphere created in the Frankenstein passage. In the final two stanzas, it is revealed that the rain, despite its initial portrayal as playful and comparable to birdsong and then its reduction to nothing more than the extinguisher of the twilight, it is revealed to be the architect of rainbows. The description of the rainbow is ecstatic with allusions to the divine: 'from angels' wings in heaven' the rainbow originates, and is a dynamic light infused structure, glinting like 'sapphire, jacinth, chrysolites'. The final two lines are rather more mysterious in nature, as the onlooker of the rainbow struggles to determine where this divine creation ends and begins. This examination of perception can be compared to our perception of rain itself, which has, throughout the poem, been subject to numerous revisions and changes: beginning with a playful-like quality, then a tempestuous one, and finally a divine characteristic.

More perceptive close-reading here, possibly not ideal to spend so long on only one text but it does serve to develop the argument

In Frankenstein, there is no such journey, and rain is portrayed as oppressive. The rain is immediately introduced as 'dismal', a claustrophobic adjective evoking a sense of hopelessness. This idea is continued in the description of the rain in the final sentence as being an arbiter of bleakness. The rain 'drenches' the character, ascribing antagonistic properties to it, and the sky itself, rather than being the fair 'ledges of grey clouds' or the canvas where the glorious rainbow is painted on, is 'black and comfortless'. The void-like description of the sky gives it an empty yet oppressive quality, and portrays the rain and sky as angry, as opposed to wretchedly sad, as suggested in the poem.

In the poem and passage, rain plays decidedly different roles. Rain is not the explicit subject of either, but in the poem, it tends to play a more active role than in the passage, where it melds with birdsong, so both these share their connotations with each other. The movement conveyed in both passages is different: the poem flows much like a mountain spring, with a playful, rhythmic quality whereas the passage moves in a more fearful, jerky way, and tends towards disaster. In Frankenstein, rain is oppressive throughout the passage, and heightens the sense of claustrophobia. The poem does not have a simple opinion of the rain, and after presenting three different interpretations: rain as birdsong, rain as the quenching of the dying light, and rain as the source of the divinely beautiful rainbow, the reader is left in 'sweet uncertainty'.

A good conclusion which draws the argument together. Altogether a good essay, with a clear line of argument focusing on the rain, apt use of quotation to illustrate points and some impressive close-reading, particularly of the poem

Numerical mark: 26/30

Passages D&F

This essay will focus on passages D and F. Though these two passages differ substantially in terms of the extent to which they relate to the theme of rain, there are some interesting similarities and differences that can be extracted from them. Following this, it will be argued that passage D cannot reasonably be said to relate to the theme of rain, whereas passage F links strongly with that theme; the purpose of the inclusion of references to rain in the passages differ; and the portrayal of rain in both passages differs.

Maybe say what the texts are, or at least the authors, rather than referring to 'passage D' and 'passage F' throughout. This opening sets out that there will be an argument, but does not provide any detail of what features of either text will be relevant in the essay, or how the argument will be framed in relation to these specific texts.

Firstly, the assertion in the question that the passages are "all linked by the theme of rain" is too overstated. Though passage F clearly relates to this theme, containing several explicit references to rain and its effects, passage D contains only one reference to rain. This point itself is not an interesting feature of the passages, but it opens up a discussion of why these references are employed by the passages' respective authors.

Arguing with the question is a classic Oxbridge technique to generate an argument for an essay (and can often be very effective!), but in this test there is not really a question to argue with, and you are expected to use the details of the texts and a comparison between them to make the basis for an argument.

One important reason to focus on is what function these references perform. In passage D, "rain" acts as a metaphor for "mercy", a positive concept, whereas it is portrayed in a much more negative sense in passage F. The use of the word "rain" is a vehicle for Shakespeare to attribute divine qualities to the concept of mercy. He refers to rain, like mercy, as coming from Heaven, suggesting that mercy is a divine creation. However, in passage F, rain is used in conjunction with other negative, hellish imagery; the convict is referred to as a "Poor devil", suggesting that the rain is such a negative thing that even a criminal, compared to a creature that is used to living in Hell, should be pitied for having to endure it.

This could have been the introduction, perhaps with one more sentence on the start, as it sets up a comparison which is interesting and relevant, and suggests an actual basis for an argument. Also it has started to refer to authors rather than 'D' and 'F' which is good.

Furthermore, the portrayal of rain in the passage differs in that Shakespeare's rain is "gentle", whereas Conan Doyle's rain is far more violent. In passage F, the rain is described as "beating upon my face", suggesting that it is very violent. This could suggest that pathetic fallacy is being employed by Conan Doyle, with the violent weather foreshadowing violent events that are likely to come later in the novel. Owing to the lack of any literal rain in passage D, it cannot be said that rain is being used by Shakespeare as a form of pathetic fallacy. Rather, Shakespeare's use of this theme is more of a simple metaphor, whereas Conan Doyle's imagery is much more extended; the reference to rain is much more incidental to passage D than they are in passage F.

The suggestion of pathetic fallacy is apt and the analysis of its effect in the Conan Doyle passage is good. However I would dispute the 'simplicity' of Shakespeare's metaphor. More close-reading of that passage would be very helpful, including further quotation.

Overall, it has been argued that the two passages are similar in that they both contain references to metaphorical rain, but differ in terms of the length and content of these metaphors. Shakespeare's portrayal of rain is very positive, to the extent that is portrayed as a divine creation, and this is conveyed in a short, simple metaphor. On the other hand, Conan Doyle's description of rain is much more negative, with it being depicted as violent and hellish. The rain in passage F is, in contrast to the reference to rain in passage D, literal, though it serves a more extended figurative function through Conan Doyle's use of pathetic fallacy.

These two passages are unusually difficult to compare, and this essay does not quite succeed in drawing them together. It would be better to get straight down to the analysis and skip the preamble. Little attempt is made here to close-read the Shakespeare passage, though the reading of the Conan-Doyle passage has some good insight.

Numerical mark: 18/30

Passages B&E

In these two extracts, the rain helps to heighten both the characters' and the reader's experience of discomfort when confronted with death, but the means through which this is done in each example is varying and multi-layered.

'Varying and multi-layered' is a bit weak and unspecific, but setting up the argument as being about rain and being confronted with death is a really promising opening.

The passage from 'Wuthering Heights' opens with the rain as part of a natural and somewhat mundane or monotonous morning ("it poured down till day-dawn", "as I took my morning walk") when the narrator notices something out of place: "I observed the master's window swinging open". The sentence itself reiterates immediately the strength of the rain "driving straight in", emphasising that the open window is abnormal. So the rain sets up a logic and expectation in both us and our narrator from the outset, which is quickly overturned. This is furthered by the simple reasoning, clear punctuation, and confident conclusion of the next sentences: "He cannot be in bed, I thought: those showers would drench him through. He must either be up or out", which is again proven wrong when the narrator walks into the room to find "Mr. Heathcliff was there—laid on his back". This disproval causes discomfort because firstly the narrator's original logic was natural and made sense, making Heathcliff's presence in the room unnatural and strange. Secondly, we are reminded that our understanding of the situation, dependent as it is on the narrator's perceptions, can easily be flawed, particularly when it comes to the unpredictable character of Heathcliff. His instability and our trepidation are thus both increased.

Some nice close-reading here but more attempt to bring the texts into conversation with one another would be ideal.

A similar setting up and subsequent undermining of expectations can be seen in the extract from 'The Great Gatsby', resulting also in a heightened sense of inconsistency and disturbance. In the lengthy opening sentence, the depiction of the rain escalates from "a thick drizzle" to "horribly black and wet" to "wet to the skin". This intensification in the language might make the rain seem illogical, but the very lack of consistency prompts us to realise that it is perhaps the narrator's own discomfort, physical and mental, that is increasing. Then, when a "man with owl-eyed glasses" appears on the scene, although the narrator has "never seen him" since "three months before" and did not "know he knew about the funeral or even his name", the unexpectedness of this appearance causes another wave of disturbance which is made literal through his "splashing" entrance.

Good to point out the way the rain descriptions give us evidence about the character's mental state, and some better comparison, and summarising the structure of each passage works quite well.

Interestingly, the writer returns again and again in this passage to the apparent stranger, and particularly to the man's glasses, even in key sentences that mention Gatsby's body – surely the more central object of the funeral. Gatsby is continually subordinated in the structure of sentences like "The rain poured down his thick glasses and he took them off and wiped them to see the protecting canvas unrolled from Gatsby's grave", where the wiping of the glasses is given detail and priority over sight of the grave. Real sight of Gatsby is never achieved: "I tried to think about Gatsby... but he was too far away and I could only remember... Daisy" (emphasis added). We are even told that the rain is falling on Gatsby's body but we never see it, only hear of this through a bystander's comment, "Blessed are the dead that the rain falls on". Here the passage diverges drastically from 'Wuthering Heights'.

Again more attempt could have been made to bring the passages into a direct conversation or contrast, within one paragraph. However the way the rain is used to draw focus in this passage is well-described.

In 'Wuthering Heights', the narrator and the reader look right into the face of the dead Heathcliff, which is frightfully contradictory, at once "fierce" and seeming to "smile", yet actually being "perfectly still". The strong rain sharpens this contradictory scene as the window lattice "flapping to and fro" offers a contrast to Heathcliff's frozen stillness, and the dripping bedsheets to his bloodless wound. The wild but natural weather outdoors provides a foil for the disturbing, unnatural corpse which we finally see lying stiffly on the bed. In 'The Great Gatsby', Gatsby's body never comes into focus, for the narrator's perspective remains "dim" and "mumbled". The rain in this case only adds to the murkiness of the entire situation, portrayed repeatedly as an obstruction to vision and clarity upon the strange man's glasses. Yet the effects are still comparable. Through using the rain that can both sharpen and blur these passages, encourage certain expectations and overturn them, reflect discomfort yet do it through dissimilitude, the two writers heighten our sense of uncertainty, mystery, and tension, and our fear of what might be revealed when the lens comes into focus.

This paragraph is much better because both texts are present and compared directly. This comparison is well-executed and the readings of the two texts are convincing. Overall the essay contains some very good analysis and it both sets up its argument and brings it to a conclusion successfully.

Numerical mark: 25/30

Reading List

To supplement the materials in this book, there are a few primary and secondary texts that we recommend as preparation for the ELAT.

You can also reach out directly for help and suggestions from the UniAdmissions team through our website, as well as a whole range of admissions support ranging from bespoke tuition to informative blogs.

Modern Texts to supplement the Practice Papers

Ariel, (2004), Sylvia Plath
Published posthumously in 1965, *Ariel* is the best known of Path's collections. Try to get the 2004 version if you can, as it undoes a lot of the changes made by Ted Hughes, including 12 additional poems he had removed.

The Bloody Chamber, (1979), Angela Carter
A set of reimagined folk tales, *The Bloody Chamber* is an excellent set of short stories for comparing, and practicing resisting the temptation to bring outside texts into!

Cat in the Rain, (1925), Ernest Hemingway
A good example of modern indirect discourse prose style, where the narrator is somewhere between 1st and 3rd persons. Useful for adding to the rain themed paper.

Stories of your Life and Others, (2015), Ted Chiang
Part of a tidal wave of innovative science fiction coming out of China, Chiang's work sits nicely alongside the older vintage of scientific writing in the practice paper.

Christie Malry's Own Double-Entry, (1973), B.S. Johnson
Weird, modernist, and cruel, *Christie Malry* is entirely unlike the kind of novel you would read at school. At only 188 pages, a good way to find out if you like late 20th century experimental fiction or not.

Recommended Secondary Reading

Rhyme's Reason, (1981), John Hollander
Rhyme's Reason is a wittily written survey of pretty much every style of poetry in English. Hollander explains schemes, patterns, rhymes, and forms with charm and skill. If you find reading poetry difficult, or are intimidated by its complex rules, this is a great book for getting to grips with it.

Beginning Theory, (2017), Peter Barry
The sudden arrival of Theory with a capital Th is one of the biggest changes from A level to degree level English, at Cambridge especially. Barry's introduction is one of the best and clearest, as well as being regularly updated since its first publication in the 1990s.

Why Read the Classics?, (1991), Italo Calvino
Once you start studying literature full time, it can be helpful to remind yourself what the point of it all is from time to time. Calvino's defence of and argument for literature is among the best and wittiest.

Sophie's World, (1994), Jostein Gaarder
Although you're not studying philosophy, it helps a great deal to have an overview of philosophical ideas as you start to study literature. This playful novel is probably the most enjoyable way to develop some familiarity with the ideas of Plato, Descartes, and the rest of those guys.

1599: A Year in the Life of William Shakespeare, (2006), James Shapiro
For a while, viewing an author's works in the context of their lives was very unfashionable. Then it came back into fashion. Shapiro's investigation into what Shakespeare was doing from day to day while he was writing *Hamlet* is an excellent introduction to a more modern style of literary criticism, as well as being shorter and more accessible than the similar *Will in the World* by Stephen Greenblatt.

Deceit, Desire, and the Novel, (1961), Rene Girard
We mentioned literary theory earlier in this list, and so we've only chosen to include a few examples, as everyone finds different thinkers appealing. However, as a place to start, Girard's investigation of imitation, lust, and ambition is great fun. It also presents a theory so grand and all encompassing, it's a good place to start learning about the limits of theory as well as its advantages.

Other Resources

In Our Time, BBC Radio 4 and BBC Sounds
Each week Melvyn Bragg is joined by three academics to discuss topics as varied as Absolute Zero to Xenophon. The archive of hundreds of episodes, all available for free, on almost every topic imaginable, is an excellent place to start your research for almost any essay topic.

Culture Gabfest Podcast, Slate Magazine
A fortnightly look at what's going in contemporary culture, frequently featuring discussions of the latest books and book controversies. An excellent way to keep abreast of wider cultural topics, and a window into what top notch literary criticism applied to everyday topics looks and sounds like.

Very Short Introduction To..., Oxford University Press
Like *In Our Time*, the *Very Short Introduction* series is a great way into almost any topic. Reasonably priced, and rich with detail, these books are a great way to develop a sense of the contours of a subject before drilling down into the detail. The volume on *The Crusades* is particularly excellent.

Final Advice

Arrive well rested, well fed and well hydrated

The ELAT is an intensive test, so make sure you're ready for it. Ensure you get a good night's sleep before the exam (there is no point cramming) and don't miss breakfast. If you're taking water into the exam then make sure you've been to the toilet before so you don't have to leave during the exam. Make sure you're well rested and fed in order to be at your best!

Make Notes on your Essay

You may get asked questions on your essay at the interview. Given that there is sometimes more than four weeks from the ELAT to the interview, it is really important to make short notes on the essay title and your main arguments after the essay. You'll thank yourself after the interview if you do this.

Afterword

Remember that the route to a high score is your approach and practice. Don't fall into the trap that "you can't prepare for the ELAT"– this could not be further from the truth. With knowledge of the test, some useful time-saving techniques and plenty of practice you can dramatically boost your score.

Work hard, never give up and do yourself justice.

Good luck!

Acknowledgements

We would like to express our sincerest thanks to everyone who helped make this book possible, especially the Oxford and Cambridge Tutors who shared their expertise in compiling all the questions and answers.

Special thanks also go to Kate Granlund, Francesca Mencattelli, Sampurna Ganguly, David Cotter, Yasmin Freeman, Chris Born, Lucy Enderby, Mariana Barona, Mohona Sengupta, Rhys Danino, Yuchen Zhang, Sameer Aiyar-Majeed William Urukalo, Abiram Uthayakumar and Ewan Grainger.

Jenny & Rohan

About Us

Infinity Books is the publishing division of *Infinity Education*. We currently publish over 85 titles across a range of subject areas – covering specialised admissions tests, examination techniques, personal statement guides, plus everything else you need to improve your chances of getting on to competitive courses such as medicine and law, as well as into universities such as Oxford and Cambridge.

Outside of publishing we also operate a highly successful tuition division, called UniAdmissions. This company was founded in 2013 by Dr Rohan Agarwal and Dr David Salt, both Cambridge Medical graduates with several years of tutoring experience. Since then, every year, hundreds of applicants and schools work with us on our programmes. Through the programmes we offer, we deliver expert tuition, exclusive course places, online courses, best-selling textbooks and much more.

With a team of over 1,000 Oxbridge tutors and a proven track record, UniAdmissions have quickly become the UK's number one admissions company.

Visit and engage with us at:
Website (Infinity Books): www.infinitybooks.co.uk
Website (UniAdmissions): www.uniadmissions.co.uk
Facebook: www.facebook.com/uniadmissionsuk
Twitter: @infinitybooks7

Your Free Book

Thanks for purchasing this Ultimate Book. Readers like you have the power to make or break a book –hopefully you found this one useful and informative. *UniAdmissions* would love to hear about your experiences with this book. As thanks for your time we'll send you another ebook from our Ultimate Guide series absolutely <u>FREE</u>!

How to Redeem Your Free Ebook

1) Either scan the QR code or find the book you have on your Amazon purchase history or your email receipt to help find the book on Amazon.

2) On the product page at the Customer Reviews area, click 'Write a customer review'. Write your review and post it! Copy the review page or take a screen shot of the review you have left.

3) Head over to www.uniadmissions.co.uk/free-book and select your chosen free ebook!

Your ebook will then be emailed to you – it's as simple as that!
Alternatively, you can buy all the titles at

www.uniadmissions.co.uk/our-books

Printed in Great Britain
by Amazon

86842908R00063